HOME

18 knittable projects to keep you comfy

quince&co.

Quince & Co
quinceandco.com

ISBN 978-0-9852990-6-4

Printed in the United States by Franklin Printing.

TABLE OF CONTENTS

When I set out to make a book of home projects, I listed potholders, rugs, pillows, afghans, place mats, tea cozy, etc. But as the list grew, sweater ideas came to mind more naturally. It was clear that sweaters feel more like home to me than objects of décor. Home is, for me, a state of mind as much as it is a place, a culture distinct from the other countries I inhabit throughout the day. Is it the same for you?

Home is, indeed, the place where all is known, where you can find your way around in the dark. The way it smells, the particular quiet or hum of the fridge, the angle of light from a window — these signal home. You can switch on the light without having to think where it is. Your hand goes to the spoon in the drawer without having to look for it. You know the creaks in the floorboards, the feel of your bedroom rug under your toes, the pressure of water from the faucet. The thing about home is that you don't really notice it most of the time. Its familiarity is comforting. It allows you to think (or not think) about other things, free to dream and dawdle, to read, to knit, to put your feet up.

Home is where we shrug off one persona to don another, where we practice the art of eating, sleeping, puttering, relating to those closest to us. And if you're a knitter or reader, then you're well versed in the art of sitting on your couch, a method for coming home to another self.

Knitting and home go together so naturally. Not just because soft warm fabrics offer comfort and protection, but because our craft is a kind of respite, too. Once we learn to knit—once we love to knit— our hands naturally find their way to the needles with the singular satisfaction that we feel opening the front door at the end of the day. And the sweater we reach for after coat and shoes come off tells us we're home as much as familiar sights and sounds.

This book offers a few items of home décor, two pillows, an afghan, a small basket. But mostly it's a collection of comfortable sweaters, socks, slippers, what you wear when you're in your own country, what tells you you're home.

One more thing. What to name a group of projects? Placing books in the pictures in this book came naturally. And Willa Cather's My Ántonia, kept finding its way into the frame. So it seemed appropriate to name these projects after characters and places in her O Pioneers! series. Somehow the strong, competent women in those stories seemed just the right namesakes for the pieces you'll find in this book.

Home is where one starts from.

T. S. Eliot

TILLIE

yarn: chickadee
color: twig

Tillie...

a little cardigan to keep your shoulders warm

BERGSON SOCKS

yarn: puffin
colors: iceland/delft
       sabine/twig

Bergson socks for catching up on the news…

and sharing the news.

STELLA

(shown hem up)
yarn: lark
color: damson

Stella...

*an open cardi that you can wear
two ways, hem down (shown here)
or hem up (previous page)*

LILY SLIPPER FLATS

yarn: osprey
colors: kumlien's gull
clay
petal

ANNA

yarn: piper
color: avocet
       guadalupe

TAI BASKET

yarn: puffin
colors: iceland
chanterelle
delft
bird's egg

MAGGIE

yarn: osprey
color: iceland

Maggie...

buttoned or unbuttoned
with pockets for hands

IRENE

yarn: chickadee
color: sedum

THEO

yarn: owl tweet
color: sooty

THEA

yarn: owl
color: abyssinian

LENA

yarn: owl
color: buru

NEBRASKA THROW

yarn: owl
colors: buru
      canyon

NELSE SLIPPERS

yarn: puffin
colors: kittywake/sedum
        iceland/bird's egg

PAULINA

yarn: tern
colors: dusk
stonington

ALEXANDRA TALL SOCKS

yarn: chickadee
colors: kumlien's gull
       bird's egg

LINDEN & ALDER PILLOWS

(left)
yarn: lark
color: fjord

(right)
yarn: puffin
color: twig

EDITH

yarn: owl
color: abyssinian

PATTERNS

TILLIE SHRUG

Twist stitch patterns are one of the best things in knitting. Their etched motifs are delicate and invite the eye to follow. This pattern suggests overlapping leaves, not unlike the patterns you'd see on a wooded path in the fall. On this shrug, the pattern makes a deep border that curves around the back neck. The rest of the piece is in easy stockinette stitch for a nice contrast.

Finished measurements

16 (20, 24)" [40.5 (51, 61) cm] lower back width, intended to fit 30-38 (38¼-46¼, 46½-54½)" [76-96.5 (97-117.5, 118-138) cm] bust; shown in size 16" [40.5 cm] on 33" [84 cm] model

Yarn

Chickadee by Quince & Co
(100% American wool; 181yd [166m]/50g)
• 7 (9, 11) skeins Twig 119

Needles

• One 32" circular needle (circ) in size US 9 [5.5 mm]
• One 24" circ in size US 8 [5 mm]
• One set double-pointed needles in size US 8 [5 mm]

Or size to obtain gauge

Notions

• Stitch markers (m)
• Locking stitch markers
• Tapestry needle
• Waste yarn

Gauge

20 sts and 26 rows = 4" [10 cm] in stockinette stitch with larger needle, after blocking.

Special abbreviations

sl 1 wyib: Slip 1 st purlwise with yarn in back.
LT (left twist): Skip 1 st and knit the next st through the back loop (tbl) keeping both sts on needle, knit the 2 sts together, then slip both sts from needle.
RT (right twist): K2tog leaving sts on LH needle, knit first st again, sl both sts from needle.

Left leaf stitch (multiple of 16 sts + 7)

See also chart, next page.
Row 1: (RS) *LT, (RT) two times, k3, (LT) two times, RT, k1; rep from *, end LT, (RT) two times, k1.
Row 2 and all WS rows: Purl.
Row 3: *K1, LT, (RT) two times, k1, (LT) two times, RT, k2; rep from *, end k1, LT, (RT) two times.
Row 5: *(LT) two times, RT, k3, LT, (RT) two times, k1; rep from *, end (LT) two times, RT, k1.
Row 7: *K1, (LT) two times, RT, k1, LT, (RT) two times, k2; rep from *, end k1, (LT) two times, RT.
Row 9: *(LT) three times, k3, (RT) three times, k1; rep from *, end (LT) three times, k1.
Row 11: *K1, (LT) three times, k1, (RT) three times, k2; rep from *, end k1, (LT) three times.
Row 13: Rep Row 9.
Row 15: Rep Row 7.
Row 17: Rep Row 5.
Row 19: Rep Row 3.
Row 21: Rep Row 1.
Row 23: *K1, (RT) three times, k1, (LT) three times, k2; rep from *, end k1, (RT) three times.
Row 25: *(RT) three times, k3, (LT) three times, k1, rep from *, end (RT) three times, k1.
Row 27: Rep Row 23.
Row 28: (WS) Purl.
Rep Rows 1-28 for left leaf st.

Right leaf stitch (multiple of 16 sts + 7)

Row 1: (RS) *K1, (LT) two times, RT, k1, LT, (RT) two times, k2; rep from *, end k1, (LT) two times, RT.

Row 2 and all WS rows: Purl

Row 3: *(LT) two times, RT, k3, LT, (RT) two times, k1; rep from *, end (LT) two times, RT, k1.

Row 5: *K1, LT, (RT) two times, k1, (LT) two times, RT, k2; rep from *, end k1, LT, (RT) two times.

Row 7: *LT, (RT) two times, k3, (LT) two times, RT, k1; rep from *, end LT, (RT) two times, k1.

Row 9: *K1, (RT) three times, k1, (LT) three times, k2; rep from *, end k1, (RT) three times.

Row 11: *(RT) three times, k3, (LT) three times, k1, rep from *, end (RT) three times, k1.

Row 13: Rep Row 9.

Row 15: Rep Row 7.

Row 17: Rep Row 5.

Row 19: Rep Row 3.

Row 21: Rep Row 1.

Row 23: *(LT) three times, k3, (RT) three times, k1; rep from *, end (LT) three times, k1.

Row 25: *K1, (LT) three times, k1, (RT) three times, k2; rep from *, end k1, (LT) three times.

Row 27: Rep Row 23.

Row 28: (WS) Purl.

Rep Rows 1-28 for right leaf st.

Note

Tillie is knitted from the center back in each direction to the back width. Stitches are bound off for lower back, and remaining stitches are worked to create shoulder and front. Held stitches for each front and stitches picked up in lower back edge are worked in a continuous rib along entire lower edge. Rows from front pieces are seamed to stitches from back to form side seam, and stitches are picked up around arm opening for cuff.

Key

☐ knit on RS, purl on WS

▨ RT

▨ LT

☐ pattern repeat

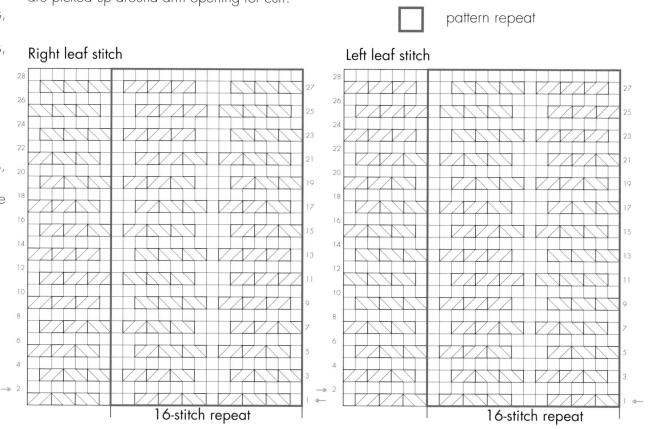

Right leaf stitch

Left leaf stitch

16-stitch repeat   16-stitch repeat

SHRUG

Begin at center back

With larger circular needle (circ) and using the long tail cast on (see page 116), CO 126 (134, 141) sts. Do not join.

Left back

First row *place marker:* (WS) P70 (78, 85) sts, place marker (pm), purl to end.

Next row: (RS) Sl 1 wyib, work Row 1 of left leaf st to marker (m), knit to end.

Next row and all WS rows: Purl.

Work in patts as est until pc meas 8 (10, 12)" [20.5 (25.5, 30.5) cm] from beg, ending after a RS row and taking note of this row of patt for working right back.

Begin left front

Next row: (WS) BO (see page 118) 35 (38, 40) sts, purl to end—91 (96, 101) sts rem.

Cont in patts until pc meas approx 16 (18½, 21)" [40.5 (47, 53.5) cm] from BO row. Place a locking stitch marker at the beg of next WS row.

Cont in patts until pc meas approx 23 (26, 29)" [58.5 (66, 73.5) cm] from BO row, ending after Row 13 or 27 and taking note of this row of patt for working right front.

Place sts onto holder or waste yarn. Do not break yarn.

Right back

With RS facing, pick up and knit 1 st in each st of CO edge—126 (134, 141) sts on needle.

First row *place marker:* (WS) Sl 1 wyib, p55, pm, purl to end.

Next row: (RS) Knit to m, work Row 1 of right leaf st to last st, p1.

Next row and all WS rows: Sl 1 wyib, purl to end.

Work in patts as est until pc meas 8 (10, 12)" [20.5 (25.5, 30.5) cm] from beg, ending after same row as for left back.

Work 1 WS row.

Begin right front

Next row: (RS) BO 35 (38, 40) sts, knit to m, work next row of patt to last st, p1—91 (96, 101) sts rem.

Cont in patts until pc meas approx 16 (18½, 21)" [40.5 (47, 53.5) cm] from BO row. Place a locking stitch marker at the beg of next RS row.

Cont in patts until pc meas approx 23 (26, 29)" [58.5 (66, 73.5) cm] from BO row, ending after same row as for left front.

Place sts onto waste yarn. Do not break yarn.

Finishing

Weave in ends. Steam- or wet-block shrug to finished measurements.

Join fronts and back and work trim

With smaller circ and RS facing, place sts for left front onto RH needle, with yarn attached to left front, pick up and knit 39 (48, 58) sts along lower edge of left back (approx 3 sts for every 4 rows), pick up and knit 1 st in center back, then pick up and knit 39 (48, 58) sts along lower edge of right back, break yarn, place sts for right front onto RH needle—261 (289, 319) sts on needle.

Beg working at right front with attached yarn.

First row: (WS) Sl 1 wyib, (p1, k1) across right front, join back, *p1, k1; rep from *, end p1.

Next row: (RS) Sl 1 wyib, *k1, p1; rep from *, end k2.

Work in rib as est for 3 more rows.

Next row: (RS) Bind off loosely in patt.

Left side seam

Beg at top of rib, and using the mattress st (see page 119), sew BO edge of left back to side edge of left front to locking st marker.

Rep for right side.

Cuff

With RS facing, using double-pointed needles, and beg at side seam, pick up and knit 70 (80, 90) sts around arm opening (approx 2 sts for every 3 rows). Pm for beg of rnd.

First rnd: *K1, p1; rep from * to end.

Cont in rib as est for 4 more rnds.

Next rnd: Bind off loosely in patt.

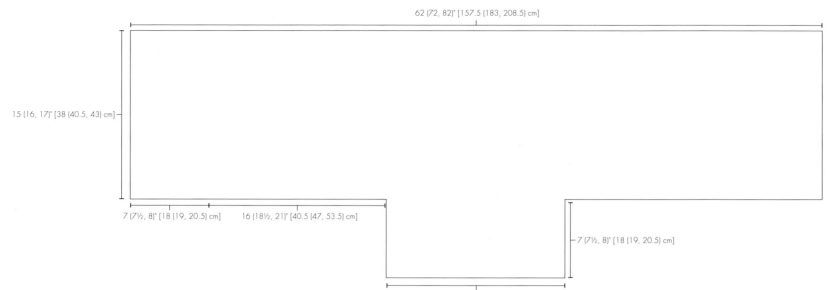

62 (72, 82)" [157.5 (183, 208.5) cm]

15 (16, 17)" [38 (40.5, 43) cm]

7 (7½, 8)" [18 (19, 20.5) cm]

16 (18½, 21)" [40.5 (47, 53.5) cm]

7 (7½, 8)" [18 (19, 20.5) cm]

16 (20, 24)" [40.5 (51, 61) cm]

Finished measurements

9¾ (11¼)" [25 (28.5) cm] cuff circumference, 8½ (9¾)" [21.5 (25) cm] foot circumference; smaller pair shown on women's size US 8, and larger on men's size US 9

Yarn

Puffin by Quince and Co

(100% American wool; 112yd [102m]/100g)

- 2 (3) skeins MC; smaller pair shown in Iceland 153 and larger in Sabine 150
- 1 skein in CC; smaller pair shown in Delft 108 and larger in Twig 119 (CC)

Note: Approx 20-25 yds of CC is used for the pair—if you have some Puffin bits in your stash, use them!

Needles

- Two 24" circular needles (circ) in size US 13 [9 mm]
- Two 24" circs in size US 15 [10 mm] (see notes)

Or size to obtain gauge

Notions

- Stitch marker (m)
- Locking stitch markers
- Tapestry needle

Gauge

11½ sts and 15 rnds = 4 " [10 cm] in stockinette stitch with larger needles, after blocking.

Special abbreviations

sl 1: Slip next stitch purlwise with yarn to the WS of work.

Notes

1. Socks are worked from cuff to toe; the heel is shaped using Japanese short rows (see page 117).
2. Socks are worked in the round on two circular needles (see page 118). The first set of stitches are given as Needle 1, the second set as Needle 2. If you prefer to use double-pointed needles (dpns), place all sts for Needle 1 onto one dpn, then evenly divide sts for Needle 2 onto two dpns.

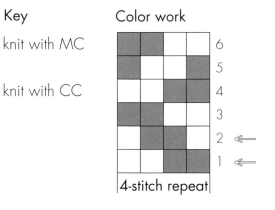

Key

☐ knit with MC

■ knit with CC

Color work

4-stitch repeat

BERGSON SOCKS

Warm and roomy, these socks pair well with popcorn and old movies. If your house is cold at night, wear them to bed. They're worked from cuff to toe with an easy non-conventional heel. For interest (and fun knitting) a simple Fair Isle pattern decorates the top of the leg.

SOCKS

Begin at cuff

With MC, using one smaller circular needle (circ) and the long tail cast on (see page 116), CO 28 (32) sts.

Arrange sts over two smaller circs as follows:

Needle 1 (N1): 14 (16) sts;
Needle 2 (N2): 14 (16) sts.

Join to work in the rnd, being careful not to twist sts. Place a locking stitch marker on the first st. Move the marker up as you work, every few rnds.

Begin ribbed border

First rnd: *K1, p1; rep from * to end.

Work 2 more rnds in rib as est.

Change to larger circs.

Next rnd: Knit.

Knit 3 more rnds.

Begin color pattern

Next rnd: Work Rnd 1 of color work chart to end.

Cont in St st and work Rnds 2-6 of color work chart.

Next rnd: Knit.

Cont in St st until sock meas 5" [13 cm] from beg.

Begin leg shaping

Left sock

Place a marker (m) at the center of sts on N2.

Next rnd *dec rnd:* (N1) Knit; (N2) Knit to 2 sts before m, k2tog, slip marker (sl m), ssk, knit to end (2 sts dec'd)—26 (30) sts rem.

Knit 5 (7) rnds.

Rep the last 6 (8) rnds one more time—24 (28) sts rem; 14 (16) sts on N1, 10 (12) sts on N2.

Rearrange stitches

Next rnd: Knit 1 st from N1, then sl this st to N2; (N1) K12 (14), knit next st onto N2; (N2) K12 (14) to end 12 (14) sts each on N1 and N2.

Next rnd: Knit across N1 only.

(Needle 2 is now Needle 1.)

Cont even in St st until sock meas 8½ (9½)" [21.5 (24) cm] from beg.

Proceed to Begin heel.

Right sock

Place a marker at the center of sts on N1.

Next rnd *dec rnd:* (N1) Knit to 2 sts before m, k2tog, sl m, ssk, knit to end (2 sts dec'd); (N2) Knit—26 (30) sts rem.

Work 5 (7) rnds even in St st.

Rep the last 6 (8) rnds one more time—24 (28) sts rem; 10 (12) sts on N1, 14 (16) sts on N2.

Rearrange stitches

Next rnd: (N1) K10 (12), knit first st from N2 onto N1; (N2) K12 (14), sl last st from N2 onto N1—12 (14) sts each on N1 and N2.

Cont even in St st until sock meas 8½ (9½)" [21.5 (24) cm] from beg.

Begin heel

Beg working back and forth on Needle 1 only.

Next row *short row 1:* (RS) Knit to last 4 (5) sts, turn, place a locking stitch marker (plm) (see page 117); (WS) Sl 1, purl to last 4 (5) sts, turn, plm.

Next row *short row 2:* (RS) Sl 1, knit to gap, pick up loop (see page 117), turn, plm; (WS) Sl 1, purl to gap, pick up loop, turn, plm.

Rep *short row two* 4 (5) more times. All sts on heel needle have been worked.

Next row: (RS) (N1) Sl 1, plm, knit to end; (N2) Pick up loop (knitting it together with first st on N2), knit to last st, sl last st to RH needle, pick up loop, return slipped st to LH needle, and k2tog (the loop and the slipped st).

Join to work in the rnd. Move marker up to mark beg of rnd.

Begin foot

Next rnd: Knit across N1 and N2.

Cont in St st until foot meas 7½ (8½)" [19 (21.5) cm] from beg of heel shaping, or 2 (2½)" [5 (6.5) cm] from desired total foot length.

Begin toe shaping

Next rnd *dec rnd:* (N1) K1, k2tog, knit to last 3 sts, ssk, k1; (N2) K1, k2tog, knit to last 3 sts, ssk, k1 (4 sts dec'd)—20 (24) sts rem.

Next rnd: Knit.

Rep the last 2 rnds 2 (3) more times—12 (16) sts rem.

Next rnd: Rep *dec rnd*—8 (12) sts rem.

Break yarn, leaving a 12" [30.5 cm] tail. Draw yarn through rem sts and cinch closed.

Finishing

Weave in ends. Steam- or wet-block socks to finished measurements.

STELLA WRAP

This wrap/shrug/cardigan is worked in a plush, open waffle stitch, a member of the brioche family. Dense as it looks, it's soft and light in the wearing. You can wear Stella in two different ways: With the armholes at the top of the piece, it makes a long, cocoon-like cardigan, turn it upside down and you have a comfy shrug with a collar to warm your neck.

Finished measurements

30½ (35½)" [77.5 (90) cm] back width from cuff to cuff, intended to fit 30-44 (44¼-58¼)" [76-112 (112.5-148) cm] bust;
shown in size 30½" [77.5 cm] on 33" [84 cm] model

Yarn

Lark by Quince & Co
(100% American wool; 134yd [123m]/50g)
*   12 (16) skeins Damson 149

Needles

*   One 32" circular needle (circ) in size US 10½ [6.5 mm]
*   One 32" circ in size US 9 [5.5 mm]

Or size to obtain gauge

Notions

*   Locking stitch markers
*   Waste yarn
*   Tapestry needle

Gauge

13 sts and 36 rows = 4" [10 cm] in double brioche stitch with larger needles, after blocking.

Special abbreviations

sl 1 wyib: Slip 1 knitwise with yarn in back.
sl1yo: Bring the yarn to the front, between the needles, then slip the next st purlwise. Leave the yarn in the front as you knit the next st (creates a yo traveling over a slipped st).
brk: Knit the next st together with its yo.

Double brioche stitch (odd number of sts)

Set up row: (WS) *K1, sl1yo; rep from *, end k1.
Row 1: (RS) *K2, sl the yo; rep from *, end k1.
Row 2: *Sl1yo, brk; rep from *, end sl1yo.
Row 3: *K1, sl the yo, k1; rep from *, end k1, sl the yo.
Row 4: *Brk, sl1yo; rep from *, end brk.
Rep Rows 1-4 for double brioche st.

Brioche stitch (odd number of sts)

Set up row: (WS) *Sl1yo, k1; rep from *, end sl1yo.
Row 1: (RS) *Brk, sl1yo; rep from *, end brk.
Row 2: *Sl1yo, brk; rep from *, end sl1yo.
Rep Rows 1 and 2 for brioche st.

Notes

1. Stella is knitted from the center back in each direction to the front length. Markers are placed as you work to guide the pick up of the lower back piece. All stitches remain live and are joined to work a continuous rib at the lower hem, then stitches are picked up along the entire front edge and worked in rib. Stitches are picked up along arm opening and worked in rib, then sides and cuffs are seamed.
2. When measuring row gauge, two rows of the pattern create one elongated "V"; one 4-row pattern repeat creates one set of two staggered Vs. To count rows, locate one V, then locate the one just slightly to the left and above this V. (This counts as four rows in pattern.) Continue counting in this manner until you've reached 4" [10 cm].
3. Throughout the piece, the first stitch of each row is slipped. When picking up stitches, each slipped edge stitch is considered one row. Remember that two rows make 1 "brioche" row, with one slipped edge stitch. So when it says to pick up 3 sts for every 4 rows, we mean for every 4 brioche rows.

WRAP

Begin at center back

With larger circular needle (circ) and using the long tail cast on (see page 116), CO 53 (59) sts. Do not join.

Left front

Set up row: (WS) P1, work Set up row for double brioche st to last st, p1.

First row: (RS) Sl 1 wyib, work Row 1 of double brioche st to last st, p1.

Next row: Sl 1 wyib, work next row of patt to last st, p1.

Cont in patt as est until pc meas 15¼ (17¾)" [38.5 (45) cm] from beg. Place a locking stitch marker at the beg of the next RS row.

Cont in patt as est until pc meas 23¾ (28)" [60.5 (71) cm] from beg, ending after Row 1.

Place sts onto waste yarn. Do not break yarn.

Right front

With RS facing and using larger circ, pick up and knit in 1 st in each CO st of left front—53 (59) sts on needle.

Work right front same as left front, placing a locking st marker at the beg of the WS row at the same measurement as for left front.

Place sts onto waste yarn. Break yarn.

Gently steam-block piece.

Back

With RS facing, using larger circ, and beg at marker on left front side edge, pick up and knit 50 (58) sts to center back (approx 3 sts for every 4 brioche rows), pick up and knit 1 st in center back, then pick up and knit 50 (58) sts to marker on right front side edge—101 (117) sts on needle.

Set up row: (WS) Sl 1 wyib, work Set up row for double brioche st to last st, p1.

First row: (RS) Sl 1 wyib, work Row 1 of double brioche st to last st, p1.

Next row: Sl 1 wyib, work next row of patt to last st, p1.

Cont in patt as est until pc meas 10½ (12¼)" [26.5 (31) cm] from pick up, ending after Row 1. Break yarn.

Join fronts and back and begin rib

With WS facing, place sts for left front, lower back, and right front onto smaller circ.

Beg working at left front with attached yarn.

Set up row: (WS) Sl 1 wyib, [sl1yo, brk] to last 2 sts on right front, sl1yo, p2tog (last right front st with first lower back st), sl1yo, [brk, sl1yo] to last back st, p2tog (last lower back st with first left front st), sl1yo, [brk, sl1yo] to last st, p1 (2 sts dec'd)—205 (233) sts on needle.

First row: (RS) Sl 1 wyib, work Row 1 of brioche st to last st, p1.

Next row: Sl 1 wyib, work next row of patt to last st, p1.

Cont in patt as est until rib meas 2" [5 cm], from pick up, ending after a WS row.

Next row: Using larger circ, bind off (see page 118) in k1, p1 rib, working first 2 sts and last 2 sts as knit sts.

Finishing

Weave in ends.   Steam- or wet-block shrug to finished measurements.

Neck trim

With RS facing, using smaller circ, and beg at lower edge of right front, pick up and knit 163 (191) sts along neck edge (approx 2 sts for every 3 brioche rows).

Set up row: (WS) Sl 1 wyib, work Set up row of brioche st to last st, p1.
First row: (RS) Sl 1 wyib, work Row 1 of brioche st to last st, p1.
Next row: Sl 1 wyib, work next row of patt to last st, p1.
Cont in patt as est until rib meas 2" [5 cm] from pick up, ending after a WS row.
Next row: (RS) Using larger circ, bind off in k1, p1 rib, working first 2 sts and last 2 sts as knit sts.

Cuff

Measure ¾" [2 cm] up each side of sleeve opening from beg of rib and place locking st markers. With RS facing, using smaller circ, and beg at marker, pick up and knit 51 (63) sts along arm opening to next m (approx 2 sts for every 3 brioche rows).

Set up row: (WS) Sl 1 wyib, work Set up row of brioche st to last st, p1.
First row: (RS) Sl 1 wyib, work Row 1 of brioche st to last st, p1.
Next row: Sl 1 wyib, work next row of patt to last st, p1.

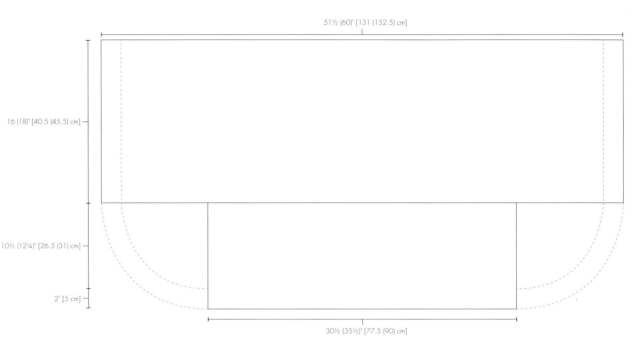

51½ (60)" [131 (152.5) cm]

16 (18)" [40.5 (45.5) cm]

10½ (12¼)" [26.5 (31) cm]

2" [5 cm]

30½ (35½)" [77.5 (90) cm]

Cont in patt as est until rib meas 2" [5 cm] from pick up, ending after a WS row.
Next row: Using larger circ, bind off in k1, p1 rib, working first 2 sts and last 2 sts as knit sts.

Rep for other cuff.
Sew side and cuff seams.

LILY SLIPPER FLATS

When you want warm feet and something pretty to put on, reach for these little slipper flats. You can knit a pair in an evening or two. This pair of Lily slippers was worked with stripes of light, sweet colors as a counter point to the main color, a conservative gray. Wouldn't the flats be great, too, in rich jewel tones—like teal and royal purple—or picture them in bright red with a bands of orange and fuchsia. Express yourself!

Finished measurements
8¼" [21 cm] long, heel to toe (unstretched), and 3½" [9 cm] heel to ankle;
shown on women's size US 8

Yarn
Osprey by Quince & Co
(100% American wool; 170yd [155m]/100g)
- 1 skein Clay 113 (A)
- 1 skein Petal 111 (B)
- 1 skein Kumlien's Gull 152 (C)

Needles
- One pair in US size 9 [5.5 mm]
- One spare needle in US size 9 [5.5 mm]

Or size to obtain gauge

Notions
- Stitch marker (m)
- Tapestry needle

Gauge
16 sts and 24 rows = 4" [10 cm] in stockinette stitch, after blocking.

Special abbreviations
m1-eyelet (make 1 eyelet): Insert LH needle from front to back under horizontal strand between st just worked and next st, knit lifted strand through the front loop (1 st increased).

Notes
Slipper flats are worked back and forth, from the ribbed edge to the center of the foot, with shaping at top of toe, and short row shaping at heel. Bottom of foot is joined using the three-needle bind off, then back of foot is sewn closed.

SLIPPERS

Begin at top edge
With A, and using the long tail cast on (see page 116), CO 62 sts.

Begin ribbed border
First row: (RS) *K1, p1; rep from * to end.
Next row: *K1, p1; rep from *.
Work in rib as est for one more row.

Begin stockinette and toe shaping
Next row: (WS) With B, p32, place marker (pm), p30.
Next row *inc row:* K2, m1, knit to 1 st before marker (m), m1-eyelet, k1, m1-eyelet, slip marker (sl m), (k1, m1-eyelet) two times, knit to end (5 sts inc'd)—67 sts.
Next row: With C, purl.
Work 2 rows even in St st.
Next row *inc row:* (RS) Knit to 3 sts before m, (k1, m1-eyelet) three times, sl m, (k1, m1-eyelet) three times, knit to end (6 sts inc'd)—73 sts.
Work 5 rows even in St st. Slipper meas approx 2½" [6.5 cm] from beg.

Begin heel and toe shaping
Next row *short row 1:* (RS) Knit to last 2 sts, w&t (see page 117); (WS) Purl to last 2 sts, w&t.
Next row *short row 2:* (RS) Knit to 7 sts before m, k2tog, k10, ssk, knit to last 3 sts, w&t; (WS) Purl to last 3 sts, w&t (2 sts dec'd).
Next row *dec row:* (RS) Knit to 7 sts before m, k2tog, k10, ssk, knit to end, picking up wraps (see page 117) (2 sts dec'd)—69 sts rem.
Next row *dec row:* Purl to 2 sts before m, p2tog, remove m, purl to end, picking up wraps (1 st dec'd)—68 sts rem.

Finishing

Weave in ends. Steam- or wet-block slippers to finished measurements.

Divide sts evenly onto two needles. With RS together and spare needle, using the three-needle bind off (see page 118), BO all sts to close bottom of slipper.

With RS facing up, sew back heel of slipper tog using the mattress stitch (see page 119).

ANNA CARDIGAN

Sometimes the perfect cardigan is long and roomy with practical pockets. Other times, it's a breezy little thing, like Anna, that barely rests on your shoulders. The sweater is knitted from the neck down with slight shaping at sides and middle fronts for a graceful bit of swing. All you do is knit, the piece is worked completely in garter stitch. It has no buttons (or buttonholes); the edges are clean and tidy and bordered by a few rows of garter stitch in a pretty, contrasting color. The sweater gets its floaty feel from Piper, a lighter-than-air yarn spun from a blend of Texas superfine mohair and merino.

Finished measurements

30½ (32¾, 35¾, 38½, 41½, 43¾, 48½, 51½, 55¼, 57½)" [77.5 (83, 91, 98, 105.5, 111, 123, 131, 140.5, 146) cm] bust circumference;

shown in size 32¾" [83 cm] with ¼" [.5 cm] of negative ease

Yarn

Piper by Quince & Co

(50% Texas superfine merino, 50% Texas super kid mohair; 305yd [279m]/50g)

- 4 (4, 4, 5, 5, 5, 5, 6, 6, 7) skeins Avocet 610 (MC)
- 1 skein Guadalupe 603 (CC)

Needles

- One 32" circular needle (circ) in size US 6 [4 mm]
- One spare needle in size US 8 [5 mm]

Or size to obtain gauge

Notions

- Stitch markers (m)
- Locking stitch marker
- Waste yarn
- Tapestry needle

Gauge

21 sts and 40 rows = 4" [10 cm] in garter stitch with smaller needle, after blocking.

Notes

1. Cardigan is knitted from the top down, with front shaping throughout. Yoke is shaped with raglan increases, and the body increased at sides, creating a fuller hip. Sleeves are worked flat from the top down, then seamed. Cuffs and hem are finished in a contrasting color, then stitches are picked up around fronts and neck to complete the contrasting trim.

2. Sleeves are worked flat to maintain accurate gauge and to avoid ladders in the garter stitch. If you prefer to work your sleeves in the round, you will need double-pointed needles. Pick up all stitches from the CO at underarm, and place marker at the center of these stitches. Knit the first round, and purl the next round to maintain garter stitch while working in the round.

3. A larger needle is used to ensure stitches aren't bound off too tightly.

4. After working a few rows, place a locking stitch marker on the RS of piece to help distinguish RS from WS.

CARDIGAN

Begin at neck

With MC, circular needle (circ), and using the long tail cast on (see page 116), CO 46 (46, 48, 51, 53, 53, 59, 61, 67, 67) sts. Do not join.

First row *place raglan markers:* (WS) K2, place marker (pm), k7, pm, k28 (28, 30, 33, 35, 35, 41, 43, 49, 49), pm, k7, pm, k2.

Next row *raglan inc row:* (RS) *Knit to 1 st before raglan marker (m), yo-inc, k1, slip marker (sl m), k1, yo-inc; rep from * three more times, knit to end (8 sts inc'd)—54 (54, 56, 59, 61, 61, 67, 69, 75, 75) sts.

Next row: Knit.

Next row *front and raglan inc row:* K1, yo-inc, k1, pm for front shaping, *yo-inc, k1, sl m, k1, yo-inc, knit to 1 st before m; rep from * two more times, yo-inc, k1, sl m, k1, yo-inc, pm for front shaping, k1, yo-inc, k1 (10 sts inc'd)—64 (64, 66, 69, 71, 71, 77, 79, 85, 85) sts.

Next row: Knit.

Next row: Rep *raglan inc row*—72 (72, 74, 77, 79, 79, 85, 87, 93, 93) sts.

Next row: Knit.

Next row *front and raglan inc row:* Knit to 1 st before front shaping m, yo-inc, k1, sl m, *knit to 1 st before raglan m, yo-inc, k1, sl m, k1, yo-inc; rep from * three more times, knit to front shaping m, sl m, k1, yo-inc, knit to end (10 sts inc'd)—82 (82, 84, 87, 89, 89, 95, 97, 103, 103) sts.

Rep the last 4 rows 4 (6, 8, 9, 9, 11, 12, 13, 14, 15) more times—154 (190, 228, 249, 251, 287, 311, 331, 355, 373) sts.

Work 3 rows even in garter st.

Next row: (RS) Rep *front and raglan inc row*—164 (200, 238, 259, 261, 297, 321, 341, 365, 383) sts.

Rep the last 4 rows 9 (8, 7, 6, 8, 7, 6, 6, 6, 7) more times—254 (280, 308, 319, 341, 367, 381, 401, 425, 453) sts.

Work 3 rows even in garter st.

Next row *front and body only inc row:* (RS) Knit to 1 st before front shaping m, yo-inc, k1, sl m, *knit to 1 st before raglan m, yo-inc, k1, sl m, knit to next raglan m, sl m, k1, yo-inc; rep from * one more time, knit to front shaping m, sl m, k1, yo-inc, knit to end (6 sts inc'd; 2 in each front, 2 in back)—260 (286, 314, 325, 347, 373, 387, 407, 431, 459) sts.

Next row: Knit.

Sizes 30½ (32¾, 35¾, 38½, 41½, 43¾, -, -, -, -)" [77.5 (83, 91, 98, 105.5, 111, -, -, -, -) cm] only

Proceed to All sizes.

Sizes - (-, -, -, -, -, 48½, 51½, 55¼, 57½)" [- (-, -, -, -, -, 123, 131, 140.5, 146) cm] only

Next row *body only inc row:* (RS) *Knit to 1 st before raglan m, yo-inc, k1, sl m, knit to next raglan m, sl m, k1, yo-inc; rep from * one more time, knit to end (4 sts inc'd; 1 in each front, 2 in back)— - (-, -, -, -, -, 391, 411, 435, 463) sts.

Next row: Knit.

Next row: Rep *front and body only inc row*— - (-, -, -, -, -, 397, 417, 441, 469) sts.

All sizes

260 (286, 314, 325, 347, 373, 397, 417, 441, 469) sts on needle; 42 (46, 50, 51, 55, 59, 63, 66, 69, 74) sts for each front, 51 (57, 63, 65, 69, 75, 77, 81, 85, 91) sts for each sleeve, and 74 (80, 88, 93, 99, 105, 117, 123, 133, 139) sts for back.

Piece meas approx 7 (7¼, 7¾, 7¾, 8½, 9, 9¼, 9¾, 10, 11)" [18 (18.5, 19.5, 19.5, 21.5, 23, 23.5, 25, 25.5, 28) cm] from beg when measured straight down at center back.

Separate fronts and back

Next row: (RS) Keeping front shaping markers on needle, *knit to raglan m, place next 51 (57, 63, 65, 69, 75, 77, 81, 85, 91) sts for sleeve onto waste yarn, using the backward loop cast on (see page 116), CO 3 (3, 3, 4, 5, 5, 5, 6, 6, 6) sts, pm for side, CO 3 (3, 3, 4, 5, 5, 5, 6, 6, 6) sts; rep from * one more time, knit to end—170 (184, 200, 211, 229, 243, 263, 279, 295, 311) sts rem on needle.

Next row: (WS) Knit.

Next row *front inc row:* Knit to 1 st before front shaping m, yo-inc, k1, sl m, knit to next front shaping m (slipping side markers), sl m, k1, yo-inc, knit to end (2 sts inc'd)—172 (186, 202, 213, 231, 245, 265, 281, 297, 313) sts.

Work 3 rows even in garter st.

Rep the last 4 rows 9 more times—190 (204, 220, 231, 249, 263, 283, 299, 315, 331) sts.

Begin side shaping

Next row *front and side inc row:* (RS) Knit to 1 st before shaping m, yo-inc, k1, sl m, *knit to 2 sts before side m, yo-inc, k2, sl m, k2, yo-inc; rep from * one more time, knit to next shaping m, sl m, k1, yo-inc, knit to end (6 sts inc'd)—196 (210, 226, 237, 255, 269, 289, 305, 321, 337) sts.

Work 3 rows even.

Next row: (RS) Rep *front inc row*—198 (212, 228, 239, 257, 271, 291, 307, 323, 339) sts.
Work 3 rows even.
Next row: (RS) Rep *front inc row*—200 (214, 230, 241, 259, 273, 293, 309, 325, 341) sts.
Work 3 rows even.
Rep the last 12 rows 5 more times—250 (264, 280, 291, 309, 323, 343, 359, 375, 391) sts; 79 (83, 87, 89, 94, 98, 102, 106, 109, 114) sts for each front and 92 (98, 106, 113, 121, 127, 139, 147, 157, 163) sts for back.
Next row: (RS) With CC, knit.
Work 2 more rows in garter st.
Next row: (WS) Using spare larger needle, bind off (see page 118) knitwise.
Piece meas approx 11½" [29 cm] from underarm.

Sleeves

With RS facing, return 51 (57, 63, 65, 69, 75, 77, 81, 85, 91) sts for sleeve to circ, and join MC.
Next row: (RS) Using the knitted cast on (see page 116), CO 4 (4, 4, 5, 6, 6, 6, 7, 7, 7) sts, knit to end.
Next row: CO 4 (4, 4, 5, 6, 6, 6, 7, 7, 7) sts, knit to end—59 (65, 71, 75, 81, 87, 89, 95, 99, 105) sts on needle.
Work 8 rows even in garter st.
Next row *dec row:* (RS) K1, k2tog, knit to last 3 sts, ssk, k1 (2 sts dec'd)—57 (63, 69, 73, 79, 85, 87, 93, 97, 103) sts rem.
Rep *dec row* every 20 (16, 14, 14, 10, 10, 10, 10, 10, 10) rows 6 (6, 9, 3, 13, 13, 13, 13, 9, 9) more times, then every 18 (14, 12, 12, 8, 8, 8, 8, 8, 8) rows 1 (3, 1, 8, 1, 1, 1, 1, 6, 6) times—43 (45, 49, 51, 51, 57, 59, 65, 67, 73) sts rem.

Work even in garter st until sleeve meas 17" [43 cm] from underarm, ending after a WS row.
Next row: (RS) With CC, knit.
Work 2 more rows in garter st.
Next row: (WS) Using spare larger needle, bind off knitwise.

Finishing

Weave in ends. Steam- or wet-block cardigan to finished measurements.
With RS facing up, sew sleeve and underarm seams using the mattress stitch (see page 119).

Trim

With CC, RS facing, and beg at lower edge of right front, pick up and knit 1 st in each garter ridge along right front, then pick up 1 st in each CO st along neck edge, then pick up and knit 1 st in each garter ridge along left front.

First row: (WS) Knit.
Next row: Knit.
Next row: (WS) Using spare larger needle, bind off knitwise.

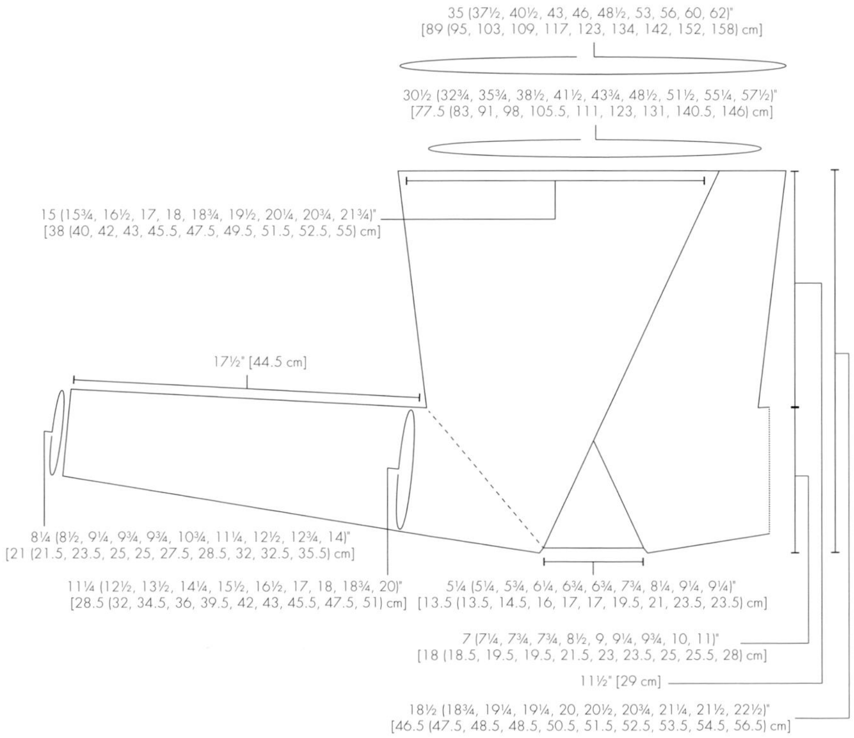

35 (37½, 40½, 43, 46, 48½, 53, 56, 60, 62)"
[89 (95, 103, 109, 117, 123, 134, 142, 152, 158) cm]
30½ (32¾, 35¾, 38½, 41½, 43¾, 48½, 51½, 55¼, 57½)"
[77.5 (83, 91, 98, 105.5, 111, 123, 131, 140.5, 146) cm]
15 (15¾, 16½, 17, 18, 18¾, 19½, 20¼, 20¾, 21¾)"
[38 (40, 42, 43, 45.5, 47.5, 49.5, 51.5, 52.5, 55) cm]
17½" [44.5 cm]
8¼ (8½, 9¼, 9¾, 9¾, 10¾, 11¼, 12½, 12¾, 14)"
[21 (21.5, 23.5, 25, 25, 27.5, 28.5, 32, 32.5, 35.5) cm]
11¼ (12½, 13½, 14¼, 15½, 16½, 17, 18, 18¾, 20)"
[28.5 (32, 34.5, 36, 39.5, 42, 43, 45.5, 47.5, 51) cm]
5¼ (5¼, 5¾, 6¼, 6¾, 6¾, 7¾, 8¼, 9¼, 9¼)"
[13.5 (13.5, 14.5, 16, 17, 17, 19.5, 21, 23.5, 23.5) cm]
7 (7¼, 7¾, 7¾, 8½, 9, 9¼, 9¾, 10, 11)"
[18 (18.5, 19.5, 19.5, 21.5, 23, 23.5, 25, 25.5, 28) cm]
11½" [29 cm]
18½ (18¾, 19¼, 19¼, 20, 20½, 20¾, 21¼, 21½, 22½)"
[46.5 (47.5, 48.5, 48.5, 50.5, 51.5, 52.5, 53.5, 54.5, 56.5) cm]

TAI BASKET

Comfort knitting, thy name is basket. Or scarf. Or garter stitch. We all have our comfort project, the one we go to when we just need to knit. I made several of these baskets but didn't think they were worth devoting a page to. Then I started combining colors. I think this little project is worth the space.

Finished measurements
24" [61 cm] circumference and 4" [10 cm] deep

Yarn
Puffin by Quince & Co
(100% American wool; 112yd [102m]/100g)
1 skein each:
- Iceland 153 (A)
- Chanterelle 118 (B)
- Delft 108 (C)
- Bird's Egg 106 (D)

Needles
- One 16" circular needle in size US 15 [10 mm]
- One set double-pointed needles (dpns) in size US 15 [10 mm]

Or size to obtain gauge

Notions
- Waste yarn
- Locking stitch marker (m)
- Tapestry needle

Gauge
9 sts and 18 rnds = 4" [10 cm] in garter stitch with yarn held double, after blocking.

Notes
Basket is knitted from the center of the base out, in the round, with yarn held double. Strands are changed one at a time, and at different points in a round, to achieve a gentle color shift.

BASKET

Begin at center of base

With one double-pointed needle (dpn) and using the waste yarn cast on (see page 117), CO 9 sts. Join working yarn, leaving a 12" [30.5 cm] tail for finishing.

First row: (RS) With one strand each of A and B, knit.
Arrange sts evenly over three dpns. Join to work in the rnd, being careful not to twist sts. Place a locking stitch marker on the first st. Move the marker up as you work, every few rnds.

Next rnd *inc rnd:* *Yo-inc, k1; rep from * to end (9 sts inc'd)—18 sts.
Next rnd: Purl.
Work 2 more rnds even in garter st.
Next rnd: Rep *inc rnd* (18 sts inc'd)—36 sts.
Next rnd: Purl.
Work 6 more rnds even in garter st.
Next rnd *inc rnd:* *Yo-inc, k2; rep from * (18 sts inc'd)—54 sts.
Change to circular needle. Move marker onto needle to mark beg of rnd.

Begin color shift

Next rnd *change color:* P15, drop B, add C, purl to end.
Work 4 rnds even in garter st.
Next rnd *change color:* Drop A, add D, knit to end.
Work 3 rnds even in garter st.

Next rnd *change color:* K8, drop C, add A, knit to end.

Work 3 rnds even in garter st.

Next rnd *change color:* K40, drop A, add B, knit to end.

Work 3 rnds even in garter st.

Next rnd *change color:* Drop C, add A, bind off (see page 118) knitwise.

Finishing

Weave in ends. Gently steam-block to shape basket.

MAGGIE CARDIGAN

Maggie is a cozy, practical sweater with pockets. A pair of branch motifs etched in twist stitches border the center front edges and embellish the top of the pockets. The cardigan knits up quickly on size US 10 needles.

Finished measurements

40½ (44, 46¼, 49¾, 52, 54¼, 57¾)" [103 (112, 117.5, 126.5, 132, 138, 146.5) cm] bust circumference, buttoned; shown in size 46¼" [117.5 cm] with 13¼" [33.5 cm] of positive ease

Yarn

Osprey by Quince & Co
(100% American wool; 170yd [155m]/100g)
• 7 (8, 8, 8, 9, 9, 10) skeins Iceland 153

Needles

• One 32" circular needle (circ) in size US 9 [5.5 mm]
• One 32" circ in size US 10 [6 mm]
• One spare needle in size US 10 [6 mm]

Or size to obtain gauge

Notions

• Stitch markers (m)
• Cable needle (cn)
• Stitch holders or waste yarn
• Tapestry needle
• Five 7/8" [22 mm] buttons

Gauge

14 sts and 22 rows = 4" [10 cm] in reverse stockinette stitch with larger needles, after blocking.

Special abbreviations

TRC-p (cross 1 twisted st right over purl): Sl 1 st onto cable needle (cn) and hold in back, k1-tbl, then p1 from cn.

TLC-p (cross 1 twisted st left over purl): Sl 1 st onto cn and hold in front, p1, then k1-tbl from cn.

Branch panel (9 sts)

See also chart, page 74.
Row 1: (RS) P3, (k1-tbl) three times, p3.
Row 2: K3, (p1-tbl) three times, k3.
Row 3: P2, TRC-p, k1-tbl, TLC-p, p2.
Row 4: K2, (p1-tbl, k1) two times, p1-tbl, k2.
Row 5: P1, TRC-p, p1, k1-tbl, p1, TLC-p, p1.
Row 6: K1, (p1-tbl, k2) two times, p1-tbl, k1.
Row 7: TRC-p, p2, k1-tbl, p2, TLC-p.
Row 8: (P1-tbl, k3) two times, p1-tbl.
Rep Rows 1-8 for branch panel.

Pocket panel (19 sts)

See also chart, page 74.
Row 1: (RS) P4, TLC-p, p3, k1-tbl, p3, TRC-p, p4.
Row 2: K5, (p1-tbl, p3) two times, p1-tbl, k5.
Row 3: P5, TLC-p, p2, k1-tbl, p2, TRC-p, p5.
Row 4: K6, (p1-tbl, p2) two times, p1-tbl, k6.
Row 5: P6, TLC-p, p1, k1-tbl, p1, TRC-p, p6.
Row 6: K7, (p1-tbl, k1) two times, p1-tbl, k7.
Row 7: P7, TLC-p, k1-tbl, TRC-p, p7.
Row 8: K8, (p1-tbl) three times, k8.
Rep Rows 1-8 for pocket panel.

Notes

Cardigan is worked in one piece from the bottom up, with v-neck shaping beginning low in the body. Stitches are bound off at the underarm, and fronts and back are worked separately to shoulders and joined using the three-needle bind off. Sleeves are worked flat, from the cuff up, and shaped with a shallow cap. Cap sts are grafted to the sides of the arm openings, then sides of cap and sleeve are seamed using the mattress stitch. Stitches are picked up for pockets, and worked up in a reversed version of the main stitch pattern, then the sides are seamed. Stitches are picked up around front edge and worked in rib with buttonholes.

CARDIGAN

Begin at hem

With smaller circular needle (circ) and using the long tail cast on (see page 116), CO 147 (159, 169, 181, 189, 199, 211) sts. Do not join.

First row: (RS) *K1, p1; rep from *, end k1.

Next row: *P1, k1; rep from *, end k1.

Work in rib until pc meas 1½" [4 cm] from beg, ending after a WS row.

Change to larger circ.

Begin reverse stockinette and branch pattern

Next row *inc/dec row:* (RS) P2, m1-p, place marker (pm) for patt, work Row 1 of branch panel over 9 sts, pm for patt, m1-p, p12 (13, 10, 11, 11, 11, 11), [p2tog, p18 (20, 16, 13, 14, 12, 13)] 5 (5, 7, 9, 9, 11, 11) times, p2tog, p11 (12, 9, 11, 10, 10, 11), m1-p, pm for patt, work Row 1 of branch panel over 9 sts, pm for patt, m1-p, p2; 4 sts inc'd and 6 (6, 8, 10, 10, 12, 12) sts dec'd—145 (157, 165, 175, 183, 191, 203) sts rem.

Next row *place side markers:* K3, work next row of panel to m, k25 (28, 30, 32, 34, 36, 39), pm for side, k71 (77, 81, 87, 91, 95, 101), pm for side, knit to panel m, work next row of panel to next m, k3.

Cont in patts as est until pc meas 10 (10, 10, 10, 10, 11½, 11½)" [25.5 (25.5, 25.5, 25.5, 25.5, 29, 29) cm] from beg, ending after a WS row.

Begin neck shaping

Next row *dec row:* (RS) P3, work next row of panel to m, sl m, ssp, purl to 2 sts before next panel m, p2tog, sl m, work next row of panel to next m, p3 to end (2 sts dec'd)—143 (155, 163, 173, 181, 189, 201) sts rem.

Work 5 (5, 5, 5, 5, 3, 3) rows even.

Rep the last 6 (6, 6, 6, 6, 4, 4) rows 4 more times, then rep *dec row* one more time—133 (145, 153, 163, 171, 179, 191) sts rem.

Work 3 rows even.

Piece meas approx 16¼ (16¼, 16¼, 16¼, 16¼, 15¾, 15¾)" [41.5 (41.5, 41.5, 41.5, 41.5, 40, 40) cm] from beg.

Separate fronts and back

Next row: (RS) *Work to 1 (2, 2, 3, 3, 4, 4) sts before side m, BO (see page 118) next 2 (4, 4, 6, 6, 8, 8) sts, removing side m; rep from * one more time, work as est to end. Break yarn.

Place 30 (32, 34, 35, 37, 38, 41) sts for each front onto holders or waste yarn—69 (73, 77, 81, 85, 87, 93) sts rem on needle for back.

Cont working on back sts only.

Back

Join yarn ready to work a WS row.

Next row: (WS) Knit.

Next row *dec row:* P3, ssp, purl to last 5 sts, p2tog, p3 (2 sts dec'd)—67 (71, 75, 79, 83, 85, 91) sts rem.

Rep *dec row* every RS row 3 (3, 4, 4, 5, 5, 7) more times—61 (65, 67, 71, 73, 75, 77) sts rem.

Work 31 (33, 33, 35, 37, 39, 39) rows even.

Piece meas approx 7 (7½, 7¾, 8¼, 9, 9¼, 10)" [18 (19, 19.5, 21, 23, 23.5, 25.5) cm] from separation of fronts and back.

Begin shoulder shaping

Next row *short row 1:* (RS) Purl to last 4 (5, 5, 3, 3, 4, 5) sts, w&t (see page 117); (WS) Knit to last 4 (5, 5, 3, 3, 4, 5) sts, w&t.

Next row *short row 2:* (RS) Purl to 3 (3, 3, 4, 4, 4, 4) sts before last wrap, w&t; (WS) Knit to 3 (3, 3, 4, 4, 4, 4) sts before last wrap, w&t.

Rep *short row 2* three more times.

Next row: (RS) Purl to end, picking up wraps (see page 117).

Next row: Knit to end, picking up wraps. Place sts onto holder or waste yarn. Break yarn.

Left front

With WS facing, return sts for left front to larger circ and join yarn.

Row 1 and all WS rows: Work in patts as est.

Row 2 *dec row 1:* (RS) P3, ssp, purl to 2 sts before m, p2tog, work as est to end (2 sts dec'd; 1 at armhole, 1 at neck edge)—28 (30, 32, 33, 35, 36, 39) sts rem.

Row 4 *dec row 2*: P3, ssp, purl to m, work as est to end (1 st dec'd)—27 (29, 31, 32, 34, 35, 38) sts rem.
Row 6: Rep *dec row 2*—26 (28, 30, 31, 33, 34, 37) sts rem.
Rep the last 6 rows 0 (0, 0, 0, 1, 1, 1) more time, then rep Rows 1-4 [0 (0, 1, 1, 0, 0, 1)] time, then rep Rows 1 and 2 [1 (1, 0, 0, 0, 0, 0)] time—24 (26, 27, 28, 29, 30, 30) sts rem.
Work 5 (5, 3, 3, 1, 1, 3) rows even.
Next row *dec row 3*: (RS) Purl to 2 sts before m, p2tog, work as est to end (1 st dec'd)—23 (25, 26, 27, 28, 29, 29) sts rem.
Work 5 rows even.
Next row: (RS) Rep *dec row 3*—22 (24, 25, 26, 27, 28, 28) sts rem.
Rep *dec row 3* every 6 rows 2 (1, 3, 3, 4, 4, 1) more times, then every 8 rows 0 (1, 0, 0, 0, 0, 2) time(s)—20 (22, 22, 23, 23, 24, 25) sts rem.
Work 7 (7, 5, 7, 5, 7, 7) rows even.
Piece meas approx 7 (7½, 7¾, 8¼, 9, 9¼, 10)" [18 (19, 19.5, 21, 23, 23.5, 25.5) cm] from separation of fronts and back.

Begin shoulder shaping

Note: When 12 sts or fewer rem to be worked after short rows, remove pattern marker and work branch panel sts in rev St st.
Next row *short row 1*: (RS) Purl to 2 sts before m, p2tog, work as est to end; (WS) Work to last 4 (5, 5, 3, 3, 4, 5) sts, w&t (1 st dec'd).
Next row *short row 2*: (RS) Work as est to end; (WS) Work to 3 (3, 3, 4, 4, 4, 4) sts before last wrap, w&t.
Rep *short row 2* three more times.
Next row: (RS) Purl to end.

Next row: Knit to end, picking up wraps—19 (21, 21, 22, 22, 23, 24) sts rem.
Place sts onto holder or waste yarn. Break yarn.

Right front

With WS facing, return sts for right front to larger circ and join yarn.
Row 1 and all WS rows: Work in patts as est.
Row 2 *dec row 1*: (RS) P3, sl m, work as est to next m, sl m, ssp, purl to last 5 sts, p2tog, p3 (2 sts dec'd; 1 at armhole, 1 at neck edge)—28 (30, 32, 33, 35, 36, 39) sts rem.
Row 4 *dec row 2*: Work as est to last 5 sts, p2tog, p3 (1 st dec'd)—27 (29, 31, 32, 34, 35, 38) sts rem.
Row 6: Rep *dec row 2*—26 (28, 30, 31, 33, 34, 37) sts rem.
Rep the last 6 rows 0 (0, 0, 0, 1, 1, 1) more time, then rep Rows 1-4 [0 (0, 1, 1, 0, 0, 1)] time, then rep Rows 1 and 2 [1 (1, 0, 0, 0, 0, 0)] time—24 (26, 27, 28, 29, 30, 30) sts rem.
Work 5 (5, 3, 3, 1, 1, 3) rows even.
Next row *dec row 3*: (RS) P3, sl m, work as est to next m, sl m, ssp, purl to end (1 st dec'd)—23 (25, 26, 27, 28, 29, 29) sts rem.
Work 5 rows even.
Next row: (RS) Rep *dec row 3*—22 (24, 25, 26, 27, 28, 28) sts rem.
Rep *dec row 3* every 6 rows 2 (1, 3, 3, 4, 4, 1) more times, then every 8 rows 0 (1, 0, 0, 0, 0, 2) time(s)—20 (22, 22, 23, 23, 24, 25) sts rem.
Work 7 (7, 5, 7, 5, 7, 7) rows even.
Piece meas approx 7 (7½, 7¾, 8¼, 9, 9¼, 10)" [18 (19, 19.5, 21, 23, 23.5, 25.5) cm] from separation of fronts and back.

Begin shoulder shaping

Next row *short row 1*: (RS) P3, sl m, work as est to next m, sl m, ssp, purl to last 4 (5, 5, 3, 3, 4, 5) sts, w&t; (WS) Work as est to end (1 st dec'd).
Next row *short row 2*: (RS) Work as est to 3 (3, 3, 4, 4, 4, 4) sts before wrap, w&t; (WS) Work as est to end.
Rep *short row 2* three more times.
Next row: (RS) Purl to end, picking up wraps—19 (21, 21, 22, 22, 23, 24) sts rem.
Next row: Knit to end.
Place sts onto holder or waste yarn. Do not break yarn.

Sleeves

With smaller circ and using the long tail cast on, CO 38 (38, 40, 40, 40, 42, 42) sts. Do not join.
First row: (RS) K2, *p1, k1; rep from * to end.
Next row: *P1, k1; rep from *, end p2.
Cont in rib as est until pc meas 1¾" [4.5 cm] from beg, ending after a WS row.
Change to larger circ.

Begin reverse stockinette

Next row *dec row*: (RS) P3, ssp, purl to last 5 sts, p2tog, p3 (2 sts dec'd)—36 (36, 38, 38, 38, 40, 40) sts rem.
Next row: Knit.
Cont in rev St st until pc meas 3¼" [8.5 cm] from beg, ending after a WS row.
Next row *inc row*: (RS) P2, m1-p, purl to last 2 sts, m1-p, p2 (2 sts inc'd)—38 (38, 40, 40, 40, 42, 42) sts.

Rep *inc row* every 12 (10, 8, 8, 6, 6, 6) rows 6 (4, 9, 3, 10, 8, 4) more times, then every 0 (8, 0, 6, 4, 4, 4) rows 0 (4, 0, 8, 3, 6, 12) times—50 (54, 58, 62, 66, 70, 74) sts. Work even until sleeve meas 18¼" [46.5 cm] from beg, ending after a WS row.

Begin cap shaping

Next row: (RS) BO 2 (3, 3, 4, 4, 5, 5) sts, purl to end.

Next row: BO 2 (3, 3, 4, 4, 5, 5) sts knit to end—46 (48, 52, 54, 58, 60, 64) sts rem.

Next row *dec row:* P3, ssp, purl to last 5 sts, p2tog, p3 (2 sts dec'd)—44 (46, 50, 52, 56, 58, 62) sts rem.

Rep *dec row* every RS row 3 (3, 4, 4, 5, 5, 7) more times—38 (40, 42, 44, 46, 48, 48) sts rem. Work 1 WS row.

Place sts onto holder or waste yarn.

Rep for other sleeve.

Join shoulders

Return sts for back to larger circ. Place sts for right front onto smaller circ. With RS together, yarn attached at right front shoulder, and spare needle, using the three-needle bind off (see page 118), BO all right front sts with back sts, BO back sts until 18 (20, 20, 21, 21, 22, 23) sts rem on LH needle, return last BO st to LH needle. Place left front sts onto smaller circ, and using the three-needle bind off, BO left front sts with rem back sts.

Finishing

Gently steam- or wet-block cardigan and sleeves to finished measurements.

Graft live sleeve cap sts (see page 118), skipping every third running thread, seam side and underarm to arm opening using the mattress stitch (see page 119).

With RS facing up, seam sleeves using the mattress stitch.

Pockets
Left pocket

Measure 3¾ (4, 4¼, 4½, 4¾, 5, 5¾)" [9.5 (10, 11, 11.5, 12, 12.5, 14.5) cm] in from left front edge. With RS facing, larger circ, and holding cardigan upside down so that the hem is facing away from you, pick up and knit 17 sts in the first purl row after rib, then, using the backward loop cast on (see page 116), CO 1 st.

First row: (RS) Purl to end, CO 1 st—19 sts on needle.

Next row: Knit.

Work in rev St st until pocket meas 2" [5 cm] from pick up, ending after a WS row.

Next row: (RS) Work Row 1 of pocket panel. Cont in patt until Rows 1–8 have been worked a total of two times.

Change to smaller circ.

Begin rib trim

Next row: (RS) K2, *p1, k1; rep from *, end k2.

Next row: P2, *k1, p1; rep from *, end p2.

Cont in rib as est for 5 more rows.

Next row: (WS) Bind off in patt.

Right pocket

Measure 3¾ (4, 4¼, 4½, 4¾, 5, 5¾)" [9.5 (10, 11, 11.5, 12, 12.5, 14.5) cm] in from right front edge, then count 17 sts past this point. Beg pick up here and work right pocket same as left.

Steam- or wet-block pockets and seam to fronts using the mattress stitch.

Buttonband

With RS facing and smaller circ, beg at bottom of right front, pick up and knit 92 (93, 95, 96, 99, 99, 101) sts (approx 2 sts for every 3 rows) along right front edge, pick up and knit 23 (23, 25, 27, 29, 29, 29) sts (1 st in each BO st) along back neck, then pick up and knit 92 (93, 95, 96, 99, 99, 101) sts along left front edge—207 (209, 215, 219, 227, 227, 231) sts on needle.

First row: (WS) *P1, k1; rep from *, end p1.

Next row *place markers:* (K1, p1) two times, k1, pm, *(p1, k1), four times, pm; rep from * 3 more times, (p1, k1) to end.

Work 1 more row in rib as est.

Next row *buttonhole row 1:* (RS) *Work in rib to m, remove m, yo2, k2tog; rep from * for each m, work in rib to end.

Next row *buttonhole row 2:* *Work in rib to buttonhole, purl into yo, dropping extra yo; rep from * for each buttonhole, work in rib to end.

Work 5 rows in rib as est.

Next row: (RS) Bind off loosely in patt.

Weave in ends. Block cardigan again, if desired.

Branch panel

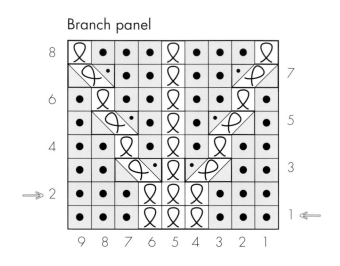

Pocket panel

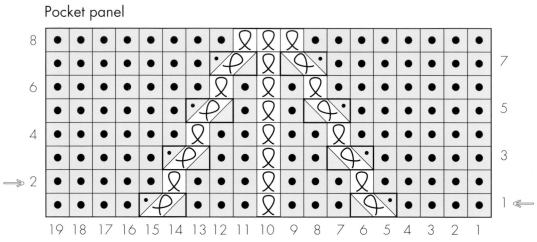

Key

 purl on RS, knit on WS

 k1-tbl on RS, p1-tbl on WS

 TRC-p

 TLC-p

74

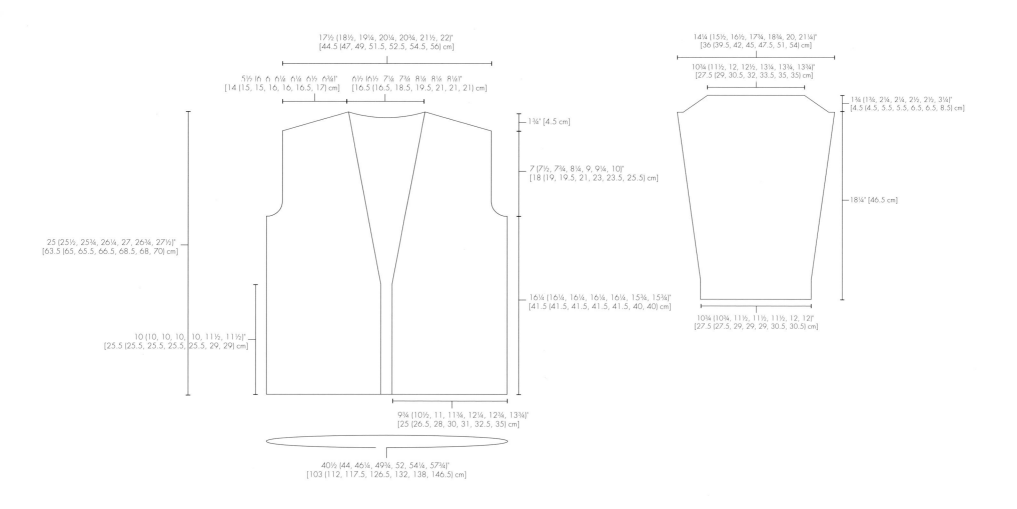

17½ (18½, 19¼, 20¼, 20¾, 21½, 22)"
[44.5 (47, 49, 51.5, 52.5, 54.5, 56) cm]

14¼ (15½, 16½, 17¾, 18¾, 20, 21¼)"
[36 (39.5, 42, 45, 47.5, 51, 54) cm]

5½ (6, 6, 6¼, 6¼, 6½, 6¾)"
[14 (15, 15, 16, 16, 16.5, 17) cm]

6½ (6½, 7¼, 7¾, 8¼, 8¼, 8¼)"
[16.5 (16.5, 18.5, 19.5, 21, 21, 21) cm]

10¾ (11½, 12, 12½, 13¼, 13¾, 13¾)"
[27.5 (29, 30.5, 32, 33.5, 35, 35) cm]

1¾" [4.5 cm]

1¾ (1¾, 2¼, 2¼, 2½, 2½, 3¼)"
[4.5 (4.5, 5.5, 5.5, 6.5, 6.5, 8.5) cm]

7 (7½, 7¾, 8¼, 9, 9¼, 10)"
[18 (19, 19.5, 21, 23, 23.5, 25.5) cm]

18¼" [46.5 cm]

25 (25½, 25¾, 26¼, 27, 26¾, 27½)"
[63.5 (65, 65.5, 66.5, 68.5, 68, 70) cm]

16¼ (16¼, 16¼, 16¼, 16¼, 15¾, 15¾)"
[41.5 (41.5, 41.5, 41.5, 41.5, 40, 40) cm]

10¾ (10¾, 11½, 11½, 11½, 12, 12)"
[27.5 (27.5, 29, 29, 29, 30.5, 30.5) cm]

10 (10, 10, 10, 10, 11½, 11½)"
[25.5 (25.5, 25.5, 25.5, 25.5, 29, 29) cm]

9¾ (10½, 11, 11¾, 12¼, 12¾, 13¾)"
[25 (26.5, 28, 30, 31, 32.5, 35) cm]

40½ (44, 46¼, 49¾, 52, 54¼, 57¾)"
[103 (112, 117.5, 126.5, 132, 138, 146.5) cm]

IRENE PULLOVER

Brioche rib is an intriguing stitch. Its deep furrows make great texture, and the doubled up stitches make a fabric that's dense, yet soft and drapey. This simple pullover dress is worked in two different brioche stitches for contrast. And it has essential pockets for carrying a Kleenex or lip balm or simply to give your hands a place to rest.

Finished measurements
40½ (43¾, 47¼, 50½, 52¼, 55½, 59)" [103 (111, 120, 128.5, 132.5, 141, 150) cm] bust circumference;
shown in size 43¾" [111 cm] with 10¾" [27.5 cm] of positive ease

Yarn
Chickadee by Quince & Co
(100% American wool; 181yd [166m]/50g)
- 12 (13, 14, 15, 16, 18, 19) skeins Sedum 142

Needles
- One 24" circular needle (circ) in size US 8 [5 mm]
- One 32" circ in size US 6 [4 mm]
- One spare circ in size US 6 [4 mm]

Or size to obtain gauge

Notions
- Stitch markers (m)
- Stitch holders or waste yarn
- Tapestry needle

Gauge
19 sts and 40 rows = 4" [10 cm] in half brioche stitch with larger needles, after blocking
19 sts and 48 rows = 4" [10 cm] in brioche stitch with smaller needles, after blocking.

Special abbreviations
sl1yo: *Before a brk:* Bring the yarn to the front, between the needles, then slip the next st purlwise. Bring the yarn over the needle, to the back, ready to knit the next st (creates a yo traveling over a slipped st).
Before a brp: With the yarn in front, slip the next st purlwise. Bring the yarn over the needle, to the back, then between the needles to the front, ready to purl the next st (creates a yo traveling over a slipped st).

brk: Knit the next st together with its yo.
brp: Purl the next st together with its yo.
sl 1 wyib: Slip the next st knitwise with yarn held in back.
br/L-dec: Slip the knit st and its yo knitwise to RH needle, knit together next purl st, knit st and its yo, then lift the slipped st and yo over the decreased st (2 sts decreased in brioche, leans to the left).
br/R-dec: Knit together the knit st, its yo, purl st, and next knit st and its yo (2 sts decreased in brioche, leans to the right).

Half brioche stitch (for swatching; odd number of sts)
Row 1: (RS) *K1, sl1yo; rep from *, end k1.
Row 2: *P1, brk; rep from *, end p1.
Rep Rows 1 and 2 for half brioche st.

Brioche stitch (for swatching; odd number of sts)
Set up row: (WS) *P1, sl1yo; rep from *, end p1.
Row 1: (RS) K1, *brk, sl1yo; rep from *, end brk, k1.
Row 2: P1, *sl1yo, brk; rep from *, end sl1yo, p1.
Rep Rows 1 and 2 for brioche st.

Notes
1. Irene is knitted from the bottom up. Front and back are worked separately to start, then joined and worked in the round to the underarm, before being separated again. The shoulders are shaped with German short rows (see page 117), and joined using the three-needle bind off.
2. Two rows in patt appear as one row, e.g. 48 rows over 4" [10 cm] looks like 24.

PULLOVER

Pockets (make 2)
With smaller circular needle (circ) and using the long tail cast on (see page 116), CO 30 sts. Do not join.

First row: (RS) Knit.

Cont in St st until pocket meas 6½" [16.5 cm] from beg, ending after a WS row.

Next row *dec row:* (RS) BO 1 st (see page 118), k13, k2tog, knit to end (2 st dec'd)—28 sts rem.

Next row: BO 1 st, *p1, sl1yo; rep from *, end p1—27 sts rem.

Place sts onto holder or waste yarn. Break yarn.

Lower Back
With larger circ and using the long tail cast on, CO 97 (105, 113, 121, 125, 133, 141) sts. Do not join.

Begin half brioche stitch
First row: (RS) Sl 1 wyib, *k1, sl1yo; rep from *, end k1, p1.

Next row: (WS) Sl 1 wyib, *p1, brk; rep from *, end p2.

Cont in patt as est until pc meas 10" [25.5 cm], ending after a WS row.

Place sts onto holder or waste yarn.

Lower Front
Work same as for back, leaving sts on needle.

Join front and back and BO for pockets
Next row *dec row:* (RS) Sl 1 wyib, k1, sl1yo, k1, BO 27 sts loosely in p1, k1 rib, [k1, sl1yo] to last 32 sts, k1, BO 27 sts loosely in p1, k1 rib, sl1yo, k1, sl last st to RH needle, return back sts to LH needle ready to work a RS row, sl last

front st to LH needle and p2tog with first back st, place marker (pm) for side, [k1, sl1yo] to last 2 sts, k1, p2tog last back st with first front st (2 sts dec'd)—138 (154, 170, 186, 194, 210, 226) sts on needle.

Pm for beg of rnd (BOR), and join to work in the rnd. (BOR is also second side marker.)

Change to smaller circ.

Insert pockets
Next rnd *set up rnd:* Sl1yo, brp, sl1yo, place sts for pocket onto LH needle ready to work a RS row, *brp, sl1yo; rep from * across pocket, then cont working [brp, sl1yo] as est to next BO, place sts for second pocket onto LH needle ready to work a RS row and cont working [brp, sl1yo] as est to BOR, end with brp—192 (208, 224, 240, 248, 264, 280) sts on needle.

Begin brioche stitch in the rnd
Rnd 1: *Brk, sl1yo; rep from *.

Rnd 2: *Sl1yo, brp; rep from *.

Rep the last 2 rnds until pc meas 17½ (17½, 17, 17, 16¾, 16¾, 16¼)" [44.5 (44.5, 43, 43, 42.5, 42.5, 41.5) cm] from beg, ending after Rnd 2.

Separate front and back
Next rnd *inc rnd:* *Using the backward loop cast on (see page 116), CO 1 st, [brk, sl1yo] to 2 sts before marker (m), brk, p1, slip marker (sl m); rep from * one more time (2 sts inc'd)—194 (210, 226, 242, 250, 266, 282) sts.

Place 97 (105, 113, 121, 125, 133, 141) sts for front onto holder or waste yarn. Work back and forth on 97 (105, 113, 121, 125, 133, 141) sts for back only.

Back
Next row: (WS) Sl 1 wyib, *sl1yo, brk; rep from * to m, end sl1yo, p1.

Next row: (RS) Sl 1 wyib, *brk, sl1yo; rep from *, end brk, p1.

Work 9 more rows as est, ending after a WS row.

Next row *inc row:* (RS) Sl 1 wyib, [brk, sl1yo] two times, (k1, yo, k1) into next st and its yo, *sl1yo, brk; rep from * to last 7 sts, sl1yo, (k1, yo, k1) into next st and its yo, [sl1yo, brk] two times, p1 (4 sts inc'd)—101 (109, 117, 125, 129, 137, 145) sts.

Next row: Sl 1 wyib, [sl1yo, brk] two times, (sl1yo, k1, sl1yo) into the inc, *brk, sl1yo; rep from * to last 9 sts, brk, (sl1yo, k1, sl1yo) into the inc, [brk, sl1yo] two times, p1.

Work 10 (12, 12, 12, 12, 12, 12) rows even. Rep the last 12 (14, 14, 14, 14, 14, 14) rows 7 (6, 7, 7, 8, 8, 9) more times, working last WS row as follows:

Next row: (WS) Sl 1 wyib, p1, *brk, sl1yo; rep from *, end brk, p2—129 (133, 145, 153, 161, 169, 181) sts.

Piece meas approx 8¾ (9, 10, 10, 11¼, 11¼, 12½)" [22 (23, 25.5, 25.5, 28.5, 28.5, 32) cm] from separation of back and front.

Begin shoulder shaping
Next row *short row 1:* (RS) Sl 1 wyib, k1, [sl1yo, brk] to last 3 sts, sl1yo, k1, turn; (WS) Make double st (see page 117), brk, p1, [brk, sl1yo] to last 3 sts, brk, p1, turn.

Next row *short row 2:* (RS) Make double st, p1, [brk, sl1yo] to 2 sts before previous double st, k1, turn; (WS) Make double st, brk, p1, [brk, sl1yo] to 3 sts before previous double st, brk, p1, turn.

Rep *short row two* 20 (21, 23, 25, 26, 28, 30) more times.

Next row *place markers:* (RS) Make double st, p1, pm, [brk, sl1yo] 19 (19, 21, 21, 23, 23, 25) times, k1, pm, p1, *k1 double st (see page 117), p1; rep from *.

Next row: (WS) Sl 1 wyib, (p1, k1) to m, [sl1yo, brk] to 1 st before next m, sl1yo, sl m, *k1, p1 double st (see page 117); rep from *, end k1, p1. Place sts onto holder or waste yarn, keeping markers in place. Break yarn.

Front

With WS facing, return sts for front to smaller circ and join yarn.

Work front as for back until beg of shoulder shaping, working last WS row as follows:

Next row *place markers:* (WS) Sl 1 wyib, p1, [brk, sl1yo] 27 (28, 31, 33, 35, 37, 40) times, brk, pm, [sl1yo, brk] 7 times, sl1yo, pm, *brk, sl1yo; rep from *, end brk, p2—129 (133, 145, 153, 161, 169, 181) sts.
Piece meas approx 8¾ (9, 10, 10, 11¼, 11¼, 12½)" [22 (23, 25.5, 25.5, 28.5, 28.5, 32) cm] from separation of back and front.

Begin neck and shoulder shaping

Note: Right and left fronts are worked simultaneously.
Next row *short row 1:* (RS) Sl 1 wyib, k1, [sl1yo, brk] to 1 st before m, p1, join a new ball of yarn and loosely bind off in k1, p1 rib to next m (removing m to work last BO), k1, [brk, sl1yo] to last 2 sts, k1, turn; (WS) Make double st, brk, p1, [brk, sl1yo] to 1 st before neck edge, p1; then sl 1 wyib, [sl1yo, brk] to last 2 sts, p1, turn.

Next row *short row 2:* (RS) Make double st, p1, [brk, sl1yo] to 2 sts before left neck edge, brk, p1; on right neck edge, sl 1 wyib, [brk, sl1yo] to 2 sts before previous double st, k1, turn; (WS) Make double st, brk, p1, [brk, sl1yo] to 1 st before neck edge, p1; then sl 1 wyib, [sl1yo, brk] to 2 sts before previous double st, p1, turn.
Rep *short row 2* one more time.

Next row *short row 3:* (RS) Make double st, p1, [brk, sl1yo] to 8 sts before neck edge, br/R-dec, [sl1yo, brk] two times, p1; then sl 1 wyib, [brk, sl1yo] two times, br/L-dec, [sl1yo, brk] to 3 sts before previous double st, sl1yo, k1, turn; (WS) Make double st, brk, p1, [brk, sl1yo] to 1 st before neck edge, p1; then sl 1 wyib, [sl1yo, brk] to 2 sts before previous double st, p1, turn (2 sts dec'd at each neck edge).
Rep *short row 2* two times, then rep *short row 3* one time (3 short rows worked and 2 sts dec'd at each neck edge).
Rep the last set of 3 short rows 4 (4, 5, 5, 6, 6, 7) more times; 19 (19, 22, 22, 25, 25, 28) total short rows worked and 12 (12, 14, 14, 16, 16, 18) sts dec'd at each neck edge.
Rep *short row two* 2 (3, 2, 4, 2, 4, 3) more times.
Next row *short row 4:* (RS) Make double st, p1, brk, p1; then sl 1 wyib, k1, turn; (WS) Make double st, p1; then sl 1 wyib, p1.
Next row: (RS) Make double st, p1; then sl 1 wyib, *k1 double st, p1; rep from *.
Next row: Sl 1 wyib, [p1, k1] to neck edge, end p2; then sl 1 wyib, *p1 double st, k1; rep from *, end p1—45 (47, 51, 55, 57, 61, 65) sts rem for each shoulder.
Do not break yarn.

Join shoulders

Place sts for back onto spare circ. With RS together, larger circ, and yarn attached at left shoulder, using the three-needle bind off (see page 118), BO all left front sts with back sts to m, remove m, loosely bind off in k1, p1 rib to next m (removing m to work last BO). Return last BO st to LH needle and using the three-needle bind off, BO all right front sts with rem back sts.

Finishing

Weave in ends. Steam- or wet-block pullover to finished measurements.
Sew pocket linings to inside of front body.

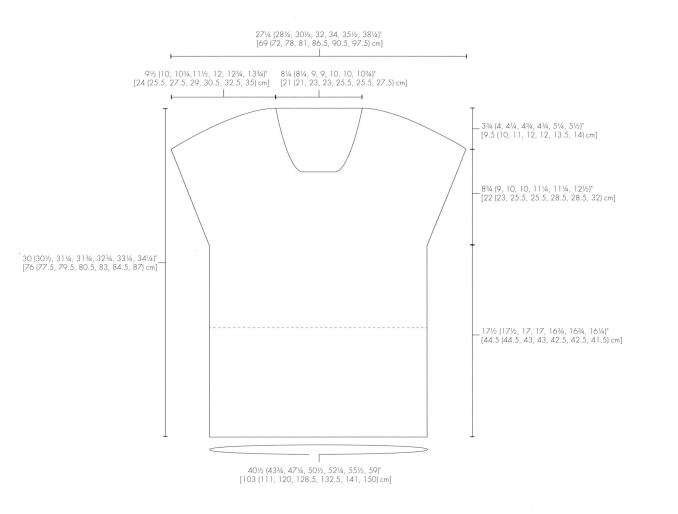

27¼ (28¼, 30½, 32, 34, 35½, 38¼)"
[69 (72, 78, 81, 86.5, 90.5, 97.5) cm]

9½ (10, 10¾,11½, 12, 12¾, 13¾)"
[24 (25.5, 27.5, 29, 30.5, 32.5, 35) cm]

8¼ (8¼, 9, 9, 10, 10, 10¾)"
[21 (21, 23, 23, 25.5, 25.5, 27.5) cm]

3¾ (4, 4¼, 4¾, 4¾, 5¼, 5½)"
[9.5 (10, 11, 12, 12, 13.5, 14) cm]

8¾ (9, 10, 10, 11¼, 11¼, 12½)"
[22 (23, 25.5, 25.5, 28.5, 28.5, 32) cm]

30 (30½, 31¼, 31¾, 32¾, 33¼, 34¼)"
[76 (77.5, 79.5, 80.5, 83, 84.5, 87) cm]

17½ (17½, 17, 17, 16¾, 16¾, 16¼)"
[44.5 (44.5, 43, 43, 42.5, 42.5, 41.5) cm]

40½ (43¾, 47¼, 50½, 52¼, 55½, 59)"
[103 (111, 120, 128.5, 132.5, 141, 150) cm]

THEO & THEA

Sometimes all you need is a torso warm up. Two strands of Owl, a buoyant wool/alpaca blend, worked in garter stitch will keep your core cozy. Note the buttons on these sweaters, they're hand carved from buffalo bones. Each one is unique. Craft on craft, that's what I love about these cushy vests.

THEA

Finished measurements

33 (35½, 39½, 42, 45½, 48, 51½, 54)" [84 (90, 100.5, 106.5, 115.5, 122, 131, 137) cm] bust circumference, buttoned; shown in size 35½" [90 cm] with 3½" [9 cm] of positive ease

Yarn

Owl by Quince & Co
(50% American wool, 50% alpaca; 120yd [110m]/50g)

- 7 (8, 9, 9, 10, 11, 12, 13) skeins Abyssinian 309

Needles

- One 32" circular needle (circ) in size US 11 [8 mm]
- One spare circ in size US 11 [8 mm]

Or size to obtain gauge

Notions

- Stitch markers (m)
- Locking stitch marker
- Stitch holders or waste yarn
- Tapestry needle
- Four 1" [25 mm] buttons

Gauge

13 sts and 22 rows = 4" [10 cm] in garter stitch held double, after blocking.

Special abbreviations

sl 1 wyib: Slip 1 st knitwise with yarn in back.

Notes

1. Vest is knitted with yarn held double, from the bottom up, in one piece. Fronts and back are separated at underarm and worked one at a time to shoulders, which are joined using the three-needle bind off. Shoulders are shaped using short rows. There is no need to pick up the wraps, as the turns are less visible in garter stitch.
2. The first stitch of every row is slipped for a tidy edge. Avoid joining new yarn at the beginning of a row to maintain this neat edge.
3. After working a few rows, place a locking stitch marker on the RS of vest to help distinguish RS from WS.

VEST

Begin at hem

With yarn held double, and using the long tail cast on (see page 116), CO 114 (122, 134, 142, 154, 162, 174, 182) sts. Do not join.

First row *place markers:* (RS) Sl 1 wyib, k29 (31, 34, 36, 39, 41, 44, 46), place marker (pm) for side, k54 (58, 64, 68, 74, 78, 84, 88), pm for side, knit to end.

Next row: Sl 1 wyib, knit to end.

Work in garter st as est until pc meas approx 4 (4, 4¼, 4¼, 4½, 5, 5¼, 5½)" [10 (10, 11, 11.5, 11.5, 12.5, 13.5, 14) cm] from beg, ending after a WS row.

Next row *buttonhole row:* (RS) Sl 1 wyib, k2, yo, k2tog, knit to end.

Work in garter st as est for 19 rows.

Next row: (RS) Rep *buttonhole row.*

Work 15 (15, 13, 11, 11, 5, 3, 1) rows even.

Piece meas approx 10½ (10½, 10½, 10½, 10¼, 9¾, 9½, 9½)" [26.5 (26.5, 26.5, 26, 26, 25, 24, 24) cm] from beg.

Separate fronts and back

Next row: (RS) Sl 1 wyib, *knit to 2 (2, 3, 3, 4, 5, 5, 5) sts before marker (m), BO (see page 118) next 4 (4, 6, 6, 8, 10, 10, 10) sts; rep from * one more time, knit to end.

Place 28 (30, 32, 34, 36, 37, 40, 42) sts for right front and 50 (54, 58, 62, 66, 68, 74, 78) sts for back onto holders or waste yarn—28 (30, 32, 34, 36, 37, 40, 42) sts rem on needle for left front.

Left front

Next row: (WS) Sl 1 wyib, knit to end.

Next row *dec row:* Sl 1 wyib, k2, ssk, knit to end (1 st dec'd)—27 (29, 31, 33, 35, 36, 39, 41) sts rem.

Rep *dec row* every RS row 5 (5, 5, 6, 7, 7, 9, 9) more times—22 (24, 26, 27, 28, 29, 30, 32) sts rem.

Work 16 (16, 18, 18, 16, 22, 20, 22) rows even.

Piece meas approx 5 (5, 5¼, 5¾, 5¾, 6¾, 7, 7½)" [12.5 (12.5, 13.5, 14.5, 14.5, 17, 18, 19) cm] from separation of fronts and back.

Begin neck shaping

Next row: (WS) BO 7 sts, knit to end—15 (17, 19, 20, 21, 22, 23, 25) sts rem.

Next row *dec row:* Sl 1 wyib, knit to last 5 sts, k2tog, k3 (1 st dec'd)—14 (16, 18, 19, 20, 21, 22, 24) sts rem.

Rep *dec row* every RS row 4 (5, 5, 6, 7, 7, 8, 9) more times—10 (11, 13, 13, 13, 14, 14, 15) sts rem.

Work 1 WS row.

Piece meas approx 7 (7½, 7¾, 8½, 9, 10, 10¾, 11½)" [18 (19, 19.5, 21.5, 23, 25.5, 27.5, 29) cm] from separation of fronts and back.

Begin shoulder shaping

Next row *short row 1:* (RS) Sl 1 wyib, knit to end; (WS) Sl 1 wyib, knit to last 3 (3, 4, 4, 4, 5, 5, 5) sts, w&t (see page 117).

Next row *short row 2:* (RS) Knit to end; (WS) Sl 1 wyib, knit to 3 (4, 4, 4, 4, 5, 5, 5) sts before last wrap, w&t.

Next row: (RS) Knit to end.

Next row: Sl 1 wyib, knit to end.

Place sts onto holder or waste yarn. Break yarn.

Right front

With WS facing, return 28 (30, 32, 34, 36, 37, 40, 42) sts for right front to circ and join yarn.

Next row: (WS) Sl 1 wyib, knit to end.

Next row *dec row:* Sl 1 wyib, knit to last 5 sts, k2tog, k3 (1 st dec'd)—27 (29, 31, 33, 35, 36, 39, 41) sts rem.

Rep *dec row* every RS row 0 (0, 1, 2, 2, 5, 6, 7) more times—27 (29, 30, 31, 33, 31, 33, 34) sts rem.

Work 1 WS row.

Next row *dec/buttonhole row:* (RS) Sl 1 wyib, k2, yo, k2tog, knit to last 5 sts, k2tog, k3 (1 st dec'd)—26 (28, 29, 30, 32, 30, 32, 33) sts rem.

Work 1 WS row.

Rep *dec row* every RS row 4 (4, 3, 3, 4, 1, 2, 1) more times—22 (24, 26, 27, 28, 29, 30, 32) sts rem.

Work 9 (9, 11, 11, 9, 15, 13, 15) rows even in garter st as est.

Next row: (RS) Rep *buttonhole row.*

Work 5 rows even.

Piece meas approx 5 (5, 5¼, 5¾, 5¾, 6¾, 7, 7½)" [12.5 (12.5, 13.5, 14.5, 14.5, 17, 18, 19) cm] from separation of fronts and back.

Begin neck shaping

Next row: (RS) BO 7 sts, knit to end—15 (17, 19, 20, 21, 22, 23, 25) sts rem.

Work 1 WS row.

Next row *dec row:* (RS) Sl 1 wyib, k2, ssk, knit to end (1 st dec'd)—14 (16, 18, 19, 20, 21, 22, 24) sts rem.

Rep *dec row* every RS row 4 (5, 5, 6, 7, 7, 8, 9) more times—10 (11, 13, 13, 13, 14, 14, 15) sts rem.

Work 1 WS row.

Piece meas approx 7 (7½, 7¾, 8½, 9, 10, 10¾, 11½)" [18 (19, 19.5, 21.5, 23, 25.5, 27.5, 29) cm] from separation of fronts and back.

Begin shoulder shaping

Next row *short row 1:* (RS) Sl 1 wyib, knit to last 3 (3, 4, 4, 4, 5, 5, 5) sts, w&t; (WS) Knit to end.

Next row *short row 2:* (RS) Sl 1 wyib, knit to 3 (4, 4, 4, 4, 5, 5, 5) sts before last wrap, w&t; (WS) Knit to end.

Next row: (RS) Knit to end.

Next row: Sl 1 wyib, knit to end.

Place sts onto holder or waste yarn. Break yarn.

Back

With WS facing, return 50 (54, 58, 62, 66, 68, 74, 78) sts for back to circ and join yarn.

Next row: (WS) Sl 1 wyib, knit to end.

Next row *dec row:* Sl 1 wyib, k2, ssk, knit to last 5 sts, k2tog, k3 (2 sts dec'd)—48 (52, 56, 60, 64, 66, 72, 76) sts rem.

Rep the last 2 rows 4 (5, 5, 6, 7, 7, 9, 9) more times—40 (42, 46, 48, 50, 52, 54, 58) sts rem.

Work 29 (29, 31, 33, 33, 39, 39, 43) rows even.

Piece meas approx 7 (7½, 7¾, 8½, 9, 10, 10¾, 11½)" [18 (19, 19.5, 21.5, 23, 25.5, 27.5, 29) cm] from separation of fronts and back.

Begin shoulder shaping

Next row *short row 1:* (RS) Sl 1 wyib, knit to last 3 (3, 4, 4, 4, 5, 5, 5) sts, w&t; (WS) Knit to last 3 (3, 4, 4, 4, 5, 5, 5) sts, w&t.

Next row *short row 2:* (RS) Knit to 3 (4, 4, 4, 4, 5, 5, 5) sts before last wrap, w&t; (WS) Knit to 3 (4, 4, 4, 4, 5, 5, 5) sts before last wrap, w&t.

Next row: (RS) Knit to end.

Next row: Sl 1 wyib, knit to end.

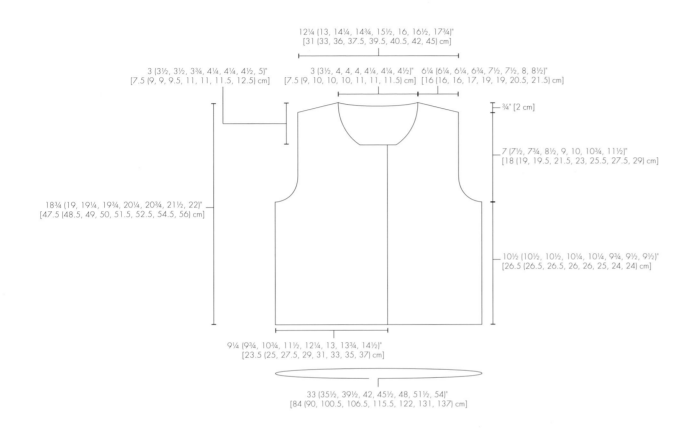

12¼ (13, 14¼, 14¾, 15½, 16, 16½, 17¾)"
[31 (33, 36, 37.5, 39.5, 40.5, 42, 45) cm]

3 (3½, 3½, 3¾, 4¼, 4¼, 4½, 5)"
[7.5 (9, 9, 9.5, 11, 11, 11.5, 12.5) cm]

3 (3½, 4, 4, 4¼, 4¼, 4½)"
[7.5 (9, 10, 10, 10, 11, 11, 11.5) cm]

6¼ (6¼, 6¼, 6¾, 7½, 7½, 8, 8½)"
[16 (16, 16, 17, 19, 19, 20.5, 21.5) cm]

¾" [2 cm]

7 (7½, 7¾, 8½, 9, 10, 10¾, 11½)"
[18 (19, 19.5, 21.5, 23, 25.5, 27.5, 29) cm]

18¾ (19, 19¼, 19¾, 20¼, 20¾, 21½, 22)"
[47.5 (48.5, 49, 50, 51.5, 52.5, 54.5, 56) cm]

10½ (10½, 10½, 10¼, 10¼, 9¾, 9½, 9½)"
[26.5 (26.5, 26.5, 26, 26, 25, 24, 24) cm]

9¼ (9¾, 10¾, 11½, 12¼, 13, 13¾, 14½)"
[23.5 (25, 27.5, 29, 31, 33, 35, 37) cm]

33 (35½, 39½, 42, 45½, 48, 51½, 54)"
[84 (90, 100.5, 106.5, 115.5, 122, 131, 137) cm]

Join shoulders

Place sts for right front onto spare circ. With RS together and using the three-needle bind off (see page 118), BO all right front sts with back sts. BO back sts until 9 (10, 12, 12, 12, 13, 13, 14) sts rem on LH needle, return last BO st to LH needle. Place sts for left front onto spare circ, with RS together and using the three-needle bind off, BO all left front sts with rem back sts.

Finishing

Weave in ends. Steam- or wet-block vest to finished measurements.
Sew buttons opposite buttonholes.

THEO

Finished measurements

35½ (39½, 42, 45½, 48, 51½, 54)" [90 (100.5, 106.5, 115.5, 122, 131, 137) cm] chest measurement, buttoned; shown in size 42" [106.5 cm] with 4½" [11.5 cm] of positive ease

Yarn

Owl Tweet by Quince & Co
(50% American wool, 50% alpaca; 120yd [110m]/50g)

- 10 (11, 11, 12, 13, 13, 14) skeins Sooty 360

Needles

- One 32" circular needle (circ) in size US 11 [8 mm]
- One spare circ in size US 11 [8 mm]

Or size to obtain gauge

Notions

- Stitch markers (m)
- Locking stitch marker
- Stitch holders or waste yarn
- Tapestry needle
- Four 1" [25 mm] buttons

Gauge

13 sts and 22 rows = 4" [10 cm] in garter stitch held double, after blocking.

Special abbreviations

sl 1 wyib: Slip 1 st knitwise with yarn in back.

Notes

1. Vest is knitted with yarn held double, from the bottom up, in one piece. Front neck shaping begins just before arm opening. Fronts and back are separated at underarm and worked one at a time to shoulders, which are joined using the three-needle bind off. Shoulders are shaped using short rows. There is no need to pick up the wraps, as the turns are less visible in garter stitch.
2. The first stitch of every row is slipped for a tidy edge. Avoid joining new yarn at the beginning of a row to maintain this neat edge.
3. After working a few rows, place a locking stitch marker on the RS of vest to help distinguish RS from WS.

VEST

Begin at hem

With yarn held double and using the long tail cast on (see page 116), CO 122 (134, 142, 154, 162, 174, 182) sts. Do not join.

First row: (RS) Sl 1 wyib, knit to end.
Next row: Sl 1 wyib, knit to end.
Rep the last 2 rows 5 more times.
Piece meas approx 2" [5 cm] from beg.
Next row buttonhole row: (RS) Sl 1 wyib, knit to last 5 sts, yo, k2tog, k3.
Work in garter st as est for 17 rows.
Rep the last 18 rows 2 more times, then rep buttonhole row one more time.
Work in garter st for 4 more rows.
Next row place side markers: (WS) Sl 1 wyib, k31 (34, 36, 39, 41, 44, 46), place marker (pm) for side, k58 (64, 68, 74, 78, 84, 88), pm for side, knit to end.
Piece meas approx 13" [33 cm] from beg.

Begin neck shaping

Next row dec row: (RS) Sl 1 wyib, k2, ssk, knit to last 5 sts, k2tog, k3 (2 sts dec'd)—120 (132, 140, 152, 160, 172, 180) sts rem.
Next row: Sl 1 wyib, knit to end.
Rep the last 2 rows 2 (2, 2, 1, 1, 0, 0) more times—116 (128, 136, 150, 158, 172, 180) sts rem.

Separate fronts and back

Next row dec row: (RS) Sl 1 wyib, k2, ssk, *knit to 2 (2, 3, 3, 4, 4, 5) sts before m, BO (see page 118) next 4 (4, 6, 6, 8, 8, 10) sts; rep from * one more time, knit to last 5 sts, k2tog, k3 (2 sts dec'd).

Place 26 (29, 30, 34, 35, 39, 40) sts for right front and 54 (60, 62, 68, 70, 76, 78) sts for back onto holders or waste yarn—26 (29, 30, 34, 35, 39, 40) sts rem on needle for left front.

Left front

Next row: (WS) Sl 1 wyib, knit to end.
Next row dec row 1: (RS) Sl 1 wyib, k2, ssk, knit to last 5 sts, k2tog, k3 (2 sts dec'd; 1 at armhole edge, 1 at neck edge)—24 (27, 28, 32, 33, 37, 38) sts rem.
Rep the last 2 rows 2 (3, 3, 5, 5, 6, 6) more times—20 (21, 22, 22, 23, 25, 26) sts rem.
Work 1 WS row.
Next row dec row 2: (RS) Sl 1 wyib, k2, ssk, knit to end (1 st dec'd)—19 (20, 21, 21, 22, 24, 25) sts rem.
Work 1 WS row.
Next row dec row 3: (RS) Sl 1 wyib, knit to last 5 sts, k2tog, k3 (1 st dec'd)—18 (19, 20, 20, 21, 23, 24) sts rem.
Work 3 rows even.
Rep the last 4 rows 5 (5, 5, 5, 5, 5, 6) more times—13 (14, 15, 15, 16, 18, 18) sts rem.
Next row: (RS) Rep dec row 3—12 (13, 14, 14, 15, 17, 17) sts rem.
Work 5 rows even, then rep dec row 3 one more time—11 (12, 13, 13, 14, 16, 16) sts rem.
Work even until pc meas 8½ (8¾, 9, 9½, 9½, 10, 10½)" [21.5 (22, 23, 24, 24, 25.5, 26.5) cm] from separation of fronts and back, ending after a WS row.

Begin shoulder shaping

Next row short row 1: (RS) Sl 1 wyib, knit to end; (WS) Sl 1 wyib, knit to last 4 (4, 5, 5, 5, 6, 6) sts, w&t (see page 117).

Next row short row 2: (RS) Knit to end; (WS) Sl 1 wyib, knit to 4 (4, 4, 4, 5, 5, 5) sts before last wrap, w&t.
Next row: (RS) Knit to end.
Next row: (WS) Sl 1, knit to end.
Place sts onto holder or waste yarn. Break yarn.

Right front

With WS facing, return 26 (29, 30, 34, 35, 39, 40) sts for right front to circ and join yarn.
Next row: (WS) Sl 1 wyib, knit to end.
Next row dec row 1: (RS) Sl 1 wyib, k2, ssk, knit to last 5 sts, k2tog, k3 (2 sts dec'd; 1 at neck edge, 1 at armhole edge)—24 (27, 28, 32, 33, 37, 38) sts rem.
Rep the last 2 rows 2 (3, 3, 5, 5, 6, 6) more times—20 (21, 22, 22, 23, 25, 26) sts rem.
Work 1 WS row.
Next row dec row 2: (RS) Sl 1 wyib, knit to last 5 sts, k2tog, k3 (1 st dec'd)—19 (20, 21, 21, 22, 24, 25) sts rem.
Work 1 WS row.
Next row dec row 3: (RS) Sl 1 wyib, k2, ssk, knit to end (1 st dec'd)—18 (19, 20, 20, 21, 23, 24) sts rem.
Work 3 rows even.
Rep the last 4 rows 5 (5, 5, 5, 5, 5, 6) more times—13 (14, 15, 15, 16, 18, 18) sts rem.
Next row: (RS) Rep dec row 3—12 (13, 14, 14, 15, 17, 17) sts rem.
Work 5 rows even, then rep dec row 3 one more time—11 (12, 13, 13, 14, 16, 16) sts rem.
Work even until pc meas 8½ (8¾, 9, 9½, 9½, 10, 10½)" [21.5 (22, 23, 24, 24, 25.5, 26.5) cm] from separation of fronts and back, ending after a WS row.

Begin shoulder shaping

Next row *short row 1:* (RS) Sl 1 wyib, knit to last 4 (4, 5, 5, 5, 6, 6) sts, w&t; (WS) Knit to end.

Next row *short row 2:* (RS) Sl 1 wyib, knit to 4 (4, 4, 4, 5, 5, 5) sts before last wrap, w&t; (WS) Knit to end.

Next row: (RS) Sl 1 wyib, knit to end.

Next row: Sl 1 wyib, knit to end.

Place sts onto holder or waste yarn. Break yarn.

Back

With WS facing, return 54 (60, 62, 68, 70, 76, 78) sts for back to circ and join yarn.

Next row: (WS) Sl 1 wyib, knit to end.

Next row *dec row:* (RS) Sl 1 wyib, k2, ssk, knit to last 5 sts, k2tog, k3 (2 sts dec'd)—52 (58, 60, 66, 68, 74, 76) sts rem.

Rep the last 2 rows 3 (4, 4, 6, 6, 7, 7) more times—46 (50, 52, 54, 56, 60, 62) sts rem.

Work even in garter st until pc meas 8½ (8¾, 9, 9½, 9½, 10, 10½)" [21.5 (22, 23, 24, 24, 25.5, 26.5) cm] from separation of fronts and back, ending after a WS row.

Begin shoulder shaping

Next row *short row 1:* (RS) Sl 1 wyib, knit to last 4 (4, 5, 5, 5, 5, 6) sts, w&t; (WS) Knit to last 4 (4, 5, 5, 5, 6, 6) sts, w&t.

Next row *short row 2:* (RS) Knit to 4 (4, 4, 4, 5, 5, 5) sts before last wrap, w&t; (WS) Knit to 4 (4, 4, 4, 5, 5, 5) sts before last wrap, w&t.

Next row: (RS) Knit to end.

Next row: (WS) Sl 1 wyib, knit to end.

Join shoulders

Place sts for right front onto spare circ. With RS together and using the three-needle bind off (see page 118), BO all right front sts with back sts. BO back sts until 10 (11, 12, 12, 13, 15, 15) sts rem on LH needle, return last BO st to LH needle. Place sts for left front onto spare circ, with RS together and using the three-needle bind off, BO all left front sts with rem back sts.

Finishing

Weave in ends. Steam- or wet-block vest to finished measurements.

Sew buttons opposite buttonholes.

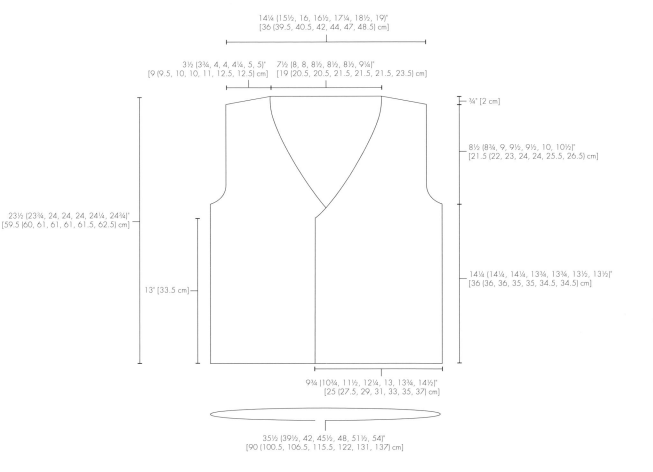

LENA SHAWL

Is it a shawl? Is it an afghan? This semi-circular throw has more room for wrapping than the traditional triangular shawl, but it isn't as cumbersome to keep positioned on the shoulders as a square afghan. A classic shell stitch pattern borders the outer edge of the piece.

Finished measurements

68" [173 cm] wingspan and 32½" [82.5 cm] deep at center

Yarn

Owl by Quince & Co

(50% American wool, 50% alpaca; 120yd [110m]/50g)

- 12 skeins Buru 310

Needles

- One 40" circular needle (circ) in size US 10½ [6.5 mm]
- One 40" circ in size US 10 [6 mm]
- One 40" circ in size US 9 [5.5 mm]

Or size to obtain gauge

Notions

- Stitch marker (m)
- Tapestry needle

Gauge

15 sts and 30 rows = 4" [10 cm] in garter stitch with smallest needle, before wet-blocking

13 sts and 27 rows = 4" [10 cm] in garter stitch with smallest needle, after wet-blocking.

Special abbreviations

sl 1 wyib: Slip one stitch purlwise with yarn in back.

s2k3p: Slip 2 sts tog knitwise to RH needle, k3tog, pass slipped st over st created by k3tog (4 sts decreased).

Shell stitch (beg and end as a multiple of 20 sts + 1)

See also chart, page 90.

Row 1: (RS) Sl 1 wyib, *(k1, p1) four times, (k1, yo) two times, (k1, p1) five times; rep from * to end (2 sts inc'd each rep).

Row 2: Sl 1 wyib, *(p1, k1) four times, p1, k3, (p1, k1) five times; rep from *, end (p1, k1) four times, p2.

Row 3: Sl 1 wyib, *(k1, p1) four times, k1, yo, k3, yo, (k1, p1) five times; rep from * (2 sts inc'd each rep).

Row 4: Sl 1 wyib, *(p1, k1) four times, p1, k5, (p1, k1) five times; rep from *, end (p1, k1) four times, p2.

Row 5: Sl 1 wyib, *(k1, p1) four times, k1, yo, k5, yo, (k1, p1) five times; rep from * (2 sts inc'd each rep).

Row 6: Sl 1 wyib, *(p1, k1) four times, p1, k7, (p1, k1) five times; rep from *, end (p1, k1) four times, p2.

Row 7: Sl 1 wyib, *(k1, p1) four times, k1, yo, k7, yo, (k1, p1) five times; rep from * (2 sts inc'd each rep).

Row 8: Sl 1 wyib, *(p1, k1) four times, p1, k9, (p1, k1) five times; rep from *, end (p1, k1) four times, p2.

Row 9: Sl 1 wyib, *(k1, p1) four times, k1, yo, k9, yo, (k1, p1) five times; rep from * (2 sts inc'd each rep).

Row 10: Sl 1 wyib, *(p1, k1) four times, p1, k11, (p1, k1) five times; rep from *, end (p1, k1) four times, p2.

Row 11: K2tog, *(k2tog) four times, k11, (ssk) four times, sk2p; rep from *, end ssk (10 sts dec'd each rep).

Row 12: Sl 1 wyib, purl to end.

Rep Rows 1-12 for shell st.

Notes

1. Shawl is worked from the bottom (long edge) up. Beginning in the pattern stitch with the largest needle and a stretchy cast on, the shawl becomes smaller first by changing needle size, then by working a decrease in the final rows of the shell pattern. Then, in garter stitch, the shawl decreases in a circular fashion until it reaches the neck edge.

2. Wet-blocking (as opposed to steam-blocking) is recommended to achieve a nicely finished shape.

SHAWL

With largest circular needle (circ) and the German twisted cast on (see page 116), CO 381 sts. Do not join.

Begin shell stitch

First row: (RS) Work Row 1 of shell st to end. Cont working in patt through Row 11. Change to next smaller circ and work Row 12. Work Rows 1-10 of patt—571 sts.

Next row dec row: (RS) K2tog, *s2k3p, k3tog, yo, k11, yo, sk2p, s2k3p, sk2p; rep from *, end ssk (12 sts dec'd each rep)—343 sts rem. Shawl meas approx 4½" [11.5 cm] from beg. Change to smallest circ.

Begin garter stitch

Next row place center marker: (WS) Sl 1 wyib, k171, place marker, k171 to end.

Next row: Sl 1 wyib, knit to end. Cont in garter st as est for 17 more rows. Shawl meas approx 7" [18 cm] from beg.

Next row dec row: (RS) Sl 1 wyib, (k2, ssk) to 2 sts before marker (m), k2, slip marker (sl m), k3, (k2tog, k2) to last st, k1 (84 sts dec'd)—259 sts rem. Work 63 rows even in garter st as est. Shawl meas approx 15½" [39.5 cm] from beg.

Begin circle decreases

Next row dec row 1: (RS) Sl 1 wyib, (k2, ssk) to m, sl m, k1, (k2tog, k2) to last st, k1 (64 sts dec'd)—195 sts rem. Work 31 rows even. Shawl meas approx 19½" [49.5 cm] from beg.

Next row dec row 2: (RS) Sl 1 wyif, (k1, ssk) to m, sl m, k1, (k2tog, k1) to last st, k1 (64 sts dec'd)—131 sts. Work 15 rows even.

Next row: (RS) Rep dec row 1 (32 sts dec'd)—99 sts rem. Work 15 rows even.

Next row: (RS) Rep dec row 2 (32 sts dec'd)—67 sts rem. Work 7 rows even.

Next row: (RS) Rep dec row 1 (16 sts dec'd)—51 sts rem. Work 7 rows even.

Next row: (RS) Rep dec row 2 (16 sts dec'd)—35 sts rem. Work 3 rows even.

Next row: (RS) Rep dec row 1 (8 sts dec'd)—27 sts rem. Work 3 rows even.

Next row: (RS) Rep dec row 2 (8 sts dec'd)—19 sts rem. Work 1 row even.

Next row dec row 3: (RS) Sl 1 wyib, (ssk) to m, sl m, k1, (k2tog) to last st, k1 (8 sts dec'd)—11 sts rem. Work 1 row even.

Next row: (RS) Rep dec row 3 (4 sts dec'd)—7 sts rem.

Next row: Knit. Slide sts to opposite end of circ. Break yarn leaving a 12" [30.5 cm] tail. Draw yarn through rem sts and cinch closed.

Finishing

Weave in ends. Wet-block shawl to finished measurements.

Shell stitch

Key

∧	sl 1 wyib
☐	knit on RS, purl on WS
●	purl on RS, knit on WS
○	yo
╱	k2tog
╲	ssk
⋏	sk2p
☐	pattern repeat
▨	no stitch

NEBRASKA THROW

Little squares worked in garter stitch mimic the patchwork of midwestern wheat fields. Deep borders of garter stitch in a strong contrasting color finish the edges top and bottom.

Finished measurements
44" [112 cm] square

Yarn
Owl by Quince & Co
(50% American wool, 50% alpaca;
120yd [110m]/50g)
- 12 skeins Buru 310 (MC)
- 4 skeins Canyon 316 (CC)

Needles
- One 40" circular needle (circ) in size US 8 [5 mm]
- One 40" circ in size US 7 [4.5 mm]

Or size to obtain gauge

Notions
- Tapestry needle

Gauge
18 sts and 27 rows = 4" [10 cm] in little squares stitch with larger needles, after blocking.

Little squares stitch (multiple of 8 sts + 3)
See also chart, next page.
Row 1 and all RS rows: Knit.
Row 2: (WS) Purl.
Row 4: *P3, k5; rep from *, end p3.
Rows 6 and 8: Rep Row 4.
Rep Rows 1-8 for little squares st.

Notes
Nebraska begins at the lower edge in contrasting trim, worked in main color in pattern stitch, then worked to upper edge in contrasting trim.

THROW

Begin garter trim
With CC, using smaller circular needle (circ) and the long tail cast on (see page 116), CO 197 sts. Do not join.

First row: (WS) Knit.
Cont in garter st until pc meas 4" [10 cm], ending after a WS row.
Change to larger circ.

Begin stitch pattern
Next row: (RS) With MC, k5, work Row 1 of little squares st to last 5 sts, k5.
Next row: K5, work next row of patt to last 5 sts, k5.
Cont in patts as est until pc meas approx 40" [101.5 cm] from beg, ending after Row 3 of patt.
Next row: (WS) Purl.
Change to smaller circ.

Begin garter trim
Next row: (RS) With CC, knit.
Cont in garter st for 4" [10 cm], ending after a WS row.
Next row: (RS) Bind off (see page 118) loosely knitwise.

Finishing
Weave in ends. Steam- or wet-block throw to finished measurements.

Key

☐	knit on RS, purl on WS
☑	purl on RS, knit on WS
☐	pattern repeat

Little squares stitch

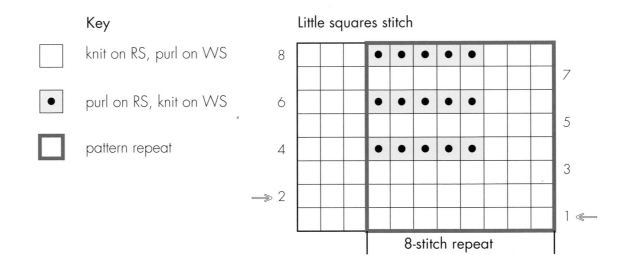

8-stitch repeat

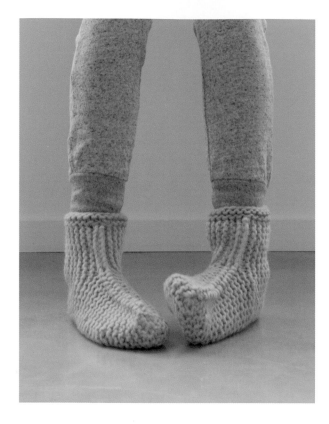

NELSE SLIPPERS

I can't resist the combination of garter stitch and chunky yarn. Warm, soft, practical slippers are the perfect vehicle for marrying the two. These are worked on size US 13 needles in no time at all. So. Need I say more?

Finished measurements
Sizes XS (S, M, L): 6½ (8, 9¾, 11¼)" [16.5 (20.5, 25, 28.5) cm], heel to toe (unstretched), 6½ (9½, 9½, 10¼)" [16.5 (24, 24, 28) cm] cuff circumference;
size M shown on women's size US 8, and size L on men's size US 9

Yarn
Puffin by Quince & Co
(100% American wool; 112yd [102m]/100g)
- 1 (2, 2, 2) skeins MC; size M shown in Iceland 153 and size L in Kittywake 151
- 1 skein CC; size M shown in Bird's Egg 106 and size L in Sedum 142

Note: Only approx 8 (11, 11, 13) yds of the CC are used per pair. If you have Puffin leftovers, use them!

Needles
- One 24" circular needle in size US 13 [9 mm]
- One set double-pointed needles (dpns) in size US 13 [9 mm]
- One spare needle in size US 15 [10 mm]

Or size to obtain gauge

Notions
- Waste yarn
- Stitch marker (m)
- Locking stitch marker
- Tapestry needle

Gauge
11 sts and 23 rows = 4" [10 cm] in garter stitch with smaller needle, after blocking.

Special abbreviations
sl 1 wyib: Slip 1 st knitwise with yarn in back.

Notes
1. Slippers are knitted flat from the back of the foot to the toe, with increases to shape the heel. Stitches are bound off at each end to create the cuff, then the piece is worked the length of the foot with decreases to shape the toe. Top of foot and front of cuff are seamed, and back of foot is closed using the three-needle bind off. Stitches are picked up around top of cuff and worked in a contrasting color.
2. After working a few rows, place a locking stitch marker on the RS of slipper to help distinguish RS from WS.

SLIPPERS

Begin at back of heel

With circular needle and using the waste yarn cast on (see page 117), CO 28 (34, 36, 42) sts. Do not join.

First row *place marker:* (RS) With MC, k14 (17, 18, 21), place marker (pm), k14 (17, 18, 21).
Next row: Sl 1 wyib, knit to end.

Begin heel shaping

Next row *inc row:* (RS) Sl 1 wyib, knit to 1 st before marker (m), yo-inc, k1, slip marker (sl m), k1, yo-inc, knit to end (2 sts inc'd)—30 (36, 38, 44) sts.
Next row: Sl 1 wyib, knit to end.
Next row *inc row:* Sl 1 wyib, knit to 2 sts before m, yo-inc, k2, sl m, k2, yo-inc, knit to end (2 sts inc'd)—32 (38, 40, 46) sts.
Next row: Sl 1 wyib, knit to end.

Size XS (-, -, -) only

Proceed to All sizes.

Sizes - (S, M, -) only

Next row *inc row:* (RS) Sl 1 wyib, knit to 3 sts before m, yo-inc, k3, sl m, k3, yo-inc, knit to end (2 sts inc'd)— - (40, 42, -) sts.
Next row: Sl 1 wyib, knit to end.
Proceed to All sizes.

Size - (-, -, L) only

Next row *inc row:* (RS) Sl 1 wyib, knit to 3 sts before m, yo-inc, k3, sl m, k3, yo-inc, knit to end (2 sts inc'd)—48 sts.
Next row: Sl 1 wyib, knit to end.
Next row *inc row:* Sl 1 wyib, knit to 4 sts before m, yo-inc, k4, sl m, k4, yo-inc, knit to end (2 sts inc'd)—50 sts.
Next row: Sl 1 wyib, knit to end.

All sizes

Cont even in garter st as est until pc meas 3¼ (4¾, 4¾, 5½)" [8.5 (12, 12, 14) cm] from beg, ending after a WS row.
Next row: (RS) BO (see page 118) 7 (8, 8 10) sts, knit to end.
Next row: BO 7 (8, 8, 10) sts, knit to end—18 (24, 26, 30) sts.
Cont even in garter st as est until pc meas 5 (6, 7½, 8¾)" [13 (15, 19, 22) cm] from beg, ending after a WS row, removing marker on last row.

Begin toe shaping

Next row *dec row:* (RS) Sl 1 wyib, k3 (5, 5, 6), ssk, k6 (8, 10, 12), k2tog, k4 (6, 6, 7) (2 sts dec'd)—16 (22, 24, 28) sts rem.
Work 5 rows in garter st as est.

Size - (S, -, -) only

Proceed to Continue toe shaping.

Sizes XS (-, M, L) only

Next row *dec row:* (RS) Sl 1 wyib, k3 (-, 5, 6), ssk, k4 (-, 8, 10), k2tog, k4 (-, 6, 7) (2 sts dec'd)— 14 (-, 22, 26) sts rem.
Next row: Sl 1 wyib, knit to end.

Continue toe shaping

Next row *dec row:* (RS) Sl 1 wyib, [ssk, k1 (3, 3, 4)] two times, [k2tog, k1 (3, 3, 4)] two times, k1 (4 sts dec'd)—10 (18, 18, 22) sts rem.

Size XS (-, -, -) only

Proceed to Finishing.

Sizes - (S, M, -) only

Next row: (WS) Sl 1 wyib, knit to end.
Next row *dec row:* Sl 1 wyib, (ssk, k2) two times, (k2tog, k2) two times, k1 (4 sts dec'd)—14 sts rem.
Next row: Sl 1 wyib, knit to end.
Next row *dec row:* Sl 1 wyib, (ssk, k1) two times, (k2tog, k1) two times, k1 (4 sts dec'd)—10 sts rem.
Proceed to Finishing.

Size - (-, -, L) only

Next row: (WS) Sl 1 wyib, knit to end.
Next row *dec row:* Sl 1 wyib, (ssk, k3) two times, (k2tog, k3) two times, k1 (4 sts dec'd)—18 sts rem.
Next row: Sl 1 wyib, knit to end.
Next row *dec row:* Sl 1 wyib, (ssk, k2) two times, (k2tog, k2) two times, k1 (4 sts dec'd)—14 sts rem.
Next row: Sl 1 wyib, knit to end.
Next row *dec row:* Sl 1 wyib, (ssk, k1) two times, (k2tog, k1) two times, k1 (4 sts dec'd)—10 sts rem.

Finishing

Break yarn leaving a 36" [91.5 cm] tail. Thread tail through rem sts and cinch closed.

Weave in ends, leaving the tail at toe for seaming. Steam- or wet-block slippers to finished measurements.

With WS facing and yarn attached at toe, sew top of foot and front of cuff using the mattress stitch (see page 119).

Pick out the waste yarn cast on (see page 117) and divide 28 (34, 36, 42) CO sts evenly onto two double-pointed needles (dpns). With MC, RS together, spare larger needle, and using the three-needle bind off (see page 118), BO all sts to close up back of slipper.

Cuff

With CC, dpns, RS facing, and beg at center back of slipper, pick up and knit 1 st in back seam, 1 st in each garter ridge, 1 st in front seam, and 1 st in each garter ridge. Place a locking st marker in center back to mark beg of rnd, and join to work in the rnd.

First rnd: Purl.

Next rnd: Knit.

Next rnd: Purl.

Next rnd: Using spare larger needle, loosely bind off knitwise.

PAULINA TEE

One requirement for an at-home sweater is that it feel free and easy, it never binds or clings or distracts from domestic pleasures. Paulina meets the criteria in spades. The sweater is a simple wide, wide rectangle with an open v-neck. When worn, the sides dip to either side in flattering points.

Finished measurements
68 (72¼, 76¾, 81)" [172.5 (183.5, 195, 205.5) cm] bust circumference;
shown in size 68" [172.5 cm] with 35" [89 cm] of positive ease
Given the oversized nature of the garment, sizes are meant to fit 30-36 (36¼-42¼, 42½-48½, 48¾-53¾)" [76-91.5 (92-107.5, 108-123, 124-136.5) cm] bust circumference.

Yarn
Tern by Quince and Co
(75% American wool, 25% silk; 221yd [202m]/50g)
- 7 (7, 8, 9) skeins Stonington 412 (MC)
- 2 skeins Dusk 415 (CC)

Needles
- One 32-48" circular needle (circ) in size US 5 [3.75 mm]
- One 24" circ in size US 4 [3.5 mm]
- One set double-pointed needles in size US 4 [3.5 mm]

Or size to obtain gauge

Notions
- Stitch markers (m)
- Waste yarn
- Tapestry needle

Gauge
22 sts and 32 rnds = 4" [10 cm] in stockinette stitch with larger needles, after blocking.
Note: Due to the nature of the fabric, sweater length may shrink by ½" [1.5 cm] after blocking.

Notes
Paulina is knitted in the round from the bottom to the beginning of front v-neck, then worked back and forth to underarm. Stitches for fronts are set aside, and back is worked to beginning of shoulder shaping. Left and right fronts are worked separately, then joined to back at shoulders. Stitches are picked up around neck and arm openings for trim.

TEE

Begin at hem

With CC, larger circular needle (circ), and using the long tail cast on (see page 116), CO 374 (398, 422, 446) sts. Place marker (pm) for beg of rnd (BOR) and join to work in the rnd, being careful not to twist sts.

First rnd *place side marker:* K187 (199, 211, 223), pm for side, knit to end. (BOR is second side marker.)
Cont in St st until pc meas 4" [10 cm] from beg.
Next rnd: With MC, knit.
Cont in St st until pc meas 13¼ (13¾, 14, 14¼)" [33.5 (35, 35.5, 36) cm] from beg.

Begin front neck shaping

Next rnd: K93 (99, 105, 111), BO (see page 118) 1 st at center front, knit to BOR, then knit to BO. Turn work—373 (397, 421, 445) sts rem.
Next row: (WS) Purl.
Next row *dec row:* K2tog, knit to last 2 sts, ssk (2 sts dec'd)—371 (395, 419, 443) sts rem.
Rep the last 2 rows 4 (2, 1, 0) more times—363 (391, 417, 443) sts rem.

Separate fronts and back

Next row: (WS) Purl to side marker (m), place sts for left front onto waste yarn, purl across back to next side m, then place sts for right front onto waste yarn—187 (199, 211, 223) sts for back rem.
Next row: Using the cable cast on (see page 116), CO 1 st, knit to end, CO 1 st—189 (201, 213, 225) sts.
Work 2 (8, 12, 16) rows even in St st.

Begin back neck shaping

Note: Left and right back pieces are worked simultaneously.

Next row: (RS) K94 (100, 106, 112), join a new ball of yarn, BO 1 st, knit to end—94 (100, 106, 112) sts rem for each side.
Next row: Purl to left neck edge; on right neck edge, purl to end.
Next row *dec row:* Knit to 2 sts before neck edge, ssk; then k2tog, knit to end (1 st dec'd at each neck edge)—93 (99, 105, 111) sts rem for each side.
Rep the last 2 rows 22 (21, 20, 20) more times—71 (78, 85, 91) sts rem for each side.

Begin shoulder and continue neck shaping

Next row *short row 1:* (RS) Knit to 2 sts before neck edge, ssk; then k2tog, knit to last 8 (7, 7, 10) sts, w&t (see page 117); (WS) Purl to neck edge; then purl to last 8 (7, 7, 10) sts, w&t (1 st dec'd at each neck edge).
Next row *short row 2:* (RS) Knit to 2 sts before neck edge, ssk; then k2tog, knit to 7 sts before last wrap, w&t; (WS) Purl to neck edge; then purl to 7 sts before last wrap, w&t (1 st dec'd at each neck edge).
Rep *short row two* 4 (5, 6, 6) more times.
Next row *short row 3:* (RS) Knit to neck edge; then knit to 7 sts before last wrap, w&t; (WS) Purl to neck edge; then purl to 7 sts before last wrap, w&t.
Next row: Rep *short row 2*—7 (7, 6, 9) sts rem at each neck edge before last wrap.
Next row: (RS) Work to neck edge; then work to end, picking up wraps (see page 117). Break yarn at left shoulder.

Next row: (WS) On right shoulder, work to neck edge, picking up wraps—64 (70, 76, 82) sts rem for each side.
Place sts onto waste yarn. Do not break yarn.

Right front

With WS facing, return sts for right front to larger circ and join yarn.
Next row: (WS) Using the cable cast on, CO 1 st, purl to end—89 (97, 104, 111) sts on needle.
Next row *dec row:* K2tog, knit to end (1 st dec'd)—88 (96, 103, 110) sts rem.
Next row: Purl.
Rep the last 2 rows 17 (19, 18, 18) more times—71 (77, 85, 92) sts rem.
Next row: (RS) Rep *dec row*—70 (76, 84, 91) sts rem.
Work 3 rows even.
Rep the last 4 rows 2 (2, 3, 4) more times—68 (74, 81, 87) sts rem.

Begin shoulder shaping

Next row *short row 1:* (RS) K2tog, knit to last 8 (7, 7, 10) sts, w&t; (WS) Purl (1 st dec'd).
Next row *short row 2:* (RS) Knit to 7 sts before last wrap, w&t; (WS) Purl.
Next row *short row 3:* (RS) K2tog, knit to 7 sts before last wrap, w&t; (WS) Purl (1 st dec'd).
Rep *short rows two* and *three* 2 (2, 3, 3) more times, then rep *short row two* 1 (2, 1, 1) times—7 (7, 6, 9) sts rem at neck edge before last wrap.
Next row: (RS) Knit to end, picking up wraps. Break yarn and place sts onto waste yarn.

Left front

With RS facing, return sts for left front to larger circ and join yarn. Using the cable cast on, CO 1 st.

Next row *dec row:* (RS) Knit to last 2 sts, ssk (1 st dec'd)—88 (96, 103, 110) sts on needle.

Next row: Purl.

Rep the last 2 rows 17 (19, 18, 18) more times—71 (77, 85, 92) sts rem.

Next row: (RS) Rep *dec row*—70 (76, 84, 91) sts rem.

Work 3 rows even.

Rep the last 4 rows 2 (2, 3, 4) more times—68 (74, 81, 87) sts rem.

Begin shoulder shaping

Next row *short row 1:* (RS) Knit to last 2 sts, ssk; (WS) Purl to last 8 (7, 7, 10) sts, w&t (1 st dec'd).

Next row *short row 2:* (RS) Knit to end; (WS) Purl to 7 sts before last wrap, w&t.

Next row *short row 3:* (RS) Knit to last 2 sts, ssk; (WS) Purl to 7 sts before last wrap, w&t (1 st dec'd).

Rep *short rows two* and *three* 2 (2, 3, 3) more times, then rep *short row two* 1 (2, 1, 1) times—7 (7, 6, 9) sts rem at neck edge before last wrap.

Next row: (RS) Knit to end.

Next row: Purl to end, picking up wraps. Do not break yarn.

Join shoulders

Place sts for left back shoulder onto smaller circ. With RS together and using the three-needle bind off (see page 118), BO all left shoulder sts.

Rep for right shoulder.

Finishing

Weave in ends. Steam- or wet-block tee to finished measurements.

Neck band

With MC, RS facing, smaller circ, and beg at right shoulder seam, pick up and knit 41 (43, 45, 51) sts along right back neck edge to center BO stitch, pick up and knit 1 st in BO, pm, pick up and knit 41 (43, 45, 51) sts along left back neck edge to left shoulder, pick up and knit 49 (51, 53, 59) sts along left front neck edge to center BO stitch, pick up and knit 1 st in BO, pm, then pick up and knit 49 (51, 53, 59) sts along right front neck edge to right shoulder—182 (190, 198, 222) sts on needle. Pm for BOR.

First rnd: Knit.

Next rnd *dec rnd:* *Knit to 3 sts before m, ssk, k1, slip marker, k2tog; rep from * one more time, knit to end (4 sts dec'd)—178 (186, 194, 218) sts rem.

Rep the last 2 rnds 5 more times—158 (166, 174, 198) sts rem.

Next rnd: Loosely bind off knitwise.

Cuff

With MC, RS facing, double-pointed needles, and beg at center of underarm, pick up and knit 33 (36, 37, 40) sts (approx 2 sts for every 3 rows) up sleeve to shoulder BO, then pick up and knit 33 (36, 37, 40) sts down sleeve to underarm—66 (72, 74, 80) sts on needles. Pm for BOR.

First rnd: Knit.

Cont in St st until cuff meas 1½" [4 cm].

Next rnd: Loosely bind off knitwise.

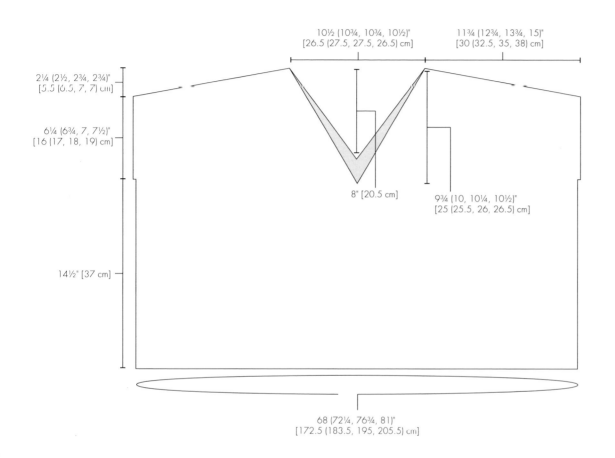

10½ (10¾, 10¾, 10½)"
[26.5 (27.5, 27.5, 26.5) cm]

11¾ (12¾, 13¾, 15)"
[30 (32.5, 35, 38) cm]

2¼ (2½, 2¾, 2¾)"
[5.5 (6.5, 7, 7) cm]

6¼ (6¾, 7, 7½)"
[16 (17, 18, 19) cm]

8" [20.5 cm]

9¾ (10, 10¼, 10½)"
[25 (25.5, 26, 26.5) cm]

14½" [37 cm]

68 (72¼, 76¾, 81)"
[172.5 (183.5, 195, 205.5) cm]

ALEXANDRA SOCKS

Squishy fisherman's rib makes a pair of cushy socks. These are worked from cuff to toe all in the same stitch, though the heel is worked in stockinette. A few inches of a contrasting color at the top of the leg makes a neat border. Alexandra socks are meant to fit loosely and be super comfortable and warm.

Finished measurements
10" [25.5 cm] calf circumference and 8" [20.5 cm] foot circumference, to fit up to 13" [33 cm] calf and women's size 7½-9½ foot;
shown on women's size US 8

Yarn
Chickadee by Quince & Co
(100% American wool; 181yd [166m]/50g)
- 3 skeins Kumlien's Gull 152 (MC)
- 1 skein Bird's Egg 106 (CC)

Needles
- Two 24" circular needles (circ) in size US 6 [4 mm] (see notes)

Or size to obtain gauge
Notions
- Locking stitch markers (m)
- Tapestry needle

Gauge
20 sts and 48 rnds = 4" [10 cm] in fisherman's rib, after blocking.

Special abbreviations
k1rb: Knit the next stitch in the row below.
p1rb: Purl the next stitch in the row below.
sl 1: Slip 1 st purlwise with yarn to the WS of work.

Fisherman's rib (even number of sts)
Rnd 1: *K1rb, p1; rep from * to end.
Rnd 2: *K1, p1rb; rep from *.
Rep Rnds 1 and 2 for fisherman's rib.

Notes
1. Socks are knitted in the round from the cuff to the toe. Calf is shaped using decreases in pattern and the shallow heel employs Japanese short rows (see page 117).
2. Two rounds in patt appear as one round, e.g. 48 rounds over 4" [10 cm] looks like 24.
3. Socks are designed to be worked in the round on two circular needles (see page 118). The first set of stitches (for calf/heel) will be given as Needle 1, and the second set (for instep) as Needle 2. Double-pointed needles are not recommended for this pattern due to the nature of the fisherman's rib stitch.

SOCKS

Begin at cuff

With CC, one circular needle (circ), and using the long tail cast on (see page 116), CO 50 sts. Arrange sts over two circs as follows:

Needle 1 (N1): 29 sts (calf);
Needle 2 (N2): 21 sts (instep).

Join to work in the rnd, being careful not to twist sts. Place a locking stitch marker on the first st. Move the marker (m) up as you work, every few rnds.

Set up rnd: *K1, p1; rep from *.
First rnd: Work Rnd 1 of fisherman's rib.
Next rnd: Work Rnd 2 of patt.
Cont in patt until sock meas 3" [7.5 cm] from beg, ending after Rnd 2.
Next rnd: With MC, work Rnd 1 of patt.
Cont in patt until sock meas 4" [10 cm] from beg, ending after Rnd 2.

Begin leg shaping

Next rnd dec rnd: (N1) Work Rnd 1 of patt over 13 sts, s2kp, beg with k1rb, cont Rnd 1 to end (2 sts dec'd)—27 sts rem; (N2) Beg with p1, cont Rnd 1 as est to end.
Next rnd: Work Rnd 2 of patt over 13 sts, p1, beg with k1, cont Rnd 2 to end.
Work even until sock meas 6" [15 cm], ending after Rnd 1.
Next rnd dec rnd: (N1) Work Rnd 2 of patt over 12 sts, k3tog, beg with p1rb, cont Rnd 2 to end (2 sts dec'd)—25 sts rem; (N2) Beg with p1rb, work Rnd 2 as est to end.
Next rnd: Work Rnd 1 of patt over 12 sts, k1, beg with p1, cont Rnd 1 to end.
Work even until sock meas 8" [20.5 cm], ending after Rnd 2.

Next rnd dec rnd: (N1) Work Rnd 1 of patt over 11 sts, s2kp, beg with k1rb, cont Rnd 1 to end (2 sts dec'd)—23 sts rem; (N2) Beg with p1, work Rnd 1 as est to end.
Next rnd: Work Rnd 2 of patt over 11 sts, p1, beg with k1, cont Rnd 2 to end.
Work even until sock meas 10" [25.5 cm], ending after Rnd 1.
Next rnd dec rnd: (N1) Work Rnd 2 of patt over 10 sts, k3tog, beg with p1rb, cont Rnd 2 to end (2 sts dec'd)—21 sts rem; (N2) Beg with p1rb, work Rnd 2 as est to end—42 total sts.
Next rnd: Work Rnd 1 of patt over 10 sts, k1, beg with p1, cont Rnd 1 to end.
Work even until sock meas 11" [28 cm], ending after Rnd 1.

Begin heel

Next rnd set up heel: (N1) Join a second strand of MC, and with yarn held double, *k1, k1rb; rep from *, end k1, break second strand; (N2) Beg with p1rb, cont Rnd 2 as est to end.
Beg working back and forth on Needle 1 only.
Next row short row 1: (RS) Join second strand of MC and with yarn held double, knit to last 7 sts, turn, place a locking stitch marker (plm) (see page 117) on double strand of yarn; (WS) Sl 1, purl to last 7 sts, turn, plm.
Next row short row 2: (RS) Sl 1, knit to gap, pick up loop (see page 117), turn, plm; (WS) Sl 1, purl to gap, pick up loop, turn, plm.
Rep short row 2 six more times. All sts on Needle 1 have been worked.

Next row: (RS) (N1) Sl 1, knit to end, break second strand; (N2) Pick up loop and purl it together with first st on N2, work Rnd 1 of patt to last st, sl last st to RH needle, pick up loop, return slipped st to LH needle, and p2tog (the loop and the slipped st).
Join to work in the rnd. Move marker up to mark beg of rnd.

Begin foot

Next rnd: (N1) *K1, p1; rep from *, end k1; (N2) P1, k1, work Rnd 2 of patt, end p1.
Next rnd: Work Rnd 1 of patt across all sts.
Work even until sock meas 6" [15 cm] from end of heel, ending after Rnd 2.

Begin toe shaping

Next rnd dec rnd: (N1) K1rb, s2kp, *k1rb, p1; rep from * to last 5 sts, k1rb, s2kp, k1rb; (N2) P1, k1rb, s2kp, *k1rb, p1; rep from * to last 6 sts, k1rb, s2kp, k1rb, p1 (8 sts dec'd)—34 sts rem.
Next rnd: (N1) K1, p1, *k1, p1rb; rep from * to last 3 sts, k1, p1, k1; (N2) P1rb, k1, p1, *k1, p1rb; rep from * to last 4 sts, k1, p1, k1, p1rb.
Next rnd: Work Rnd 1 of patt.
Next rnd: Work Rnd 2 of patt.
Rep the last 4 rnds 2 more times—18 sts rem.
Next rnd dec rnd: (N1) Ssk, (k1rb, p1) two times, k1rb, k2tog; (N2) P1, ssk, k1rb, p1, k1rb, k2tog, p1 (4 sts dec'd)—14 sts rem.
Break yarn, leaving a 12" [30.5 cm] tail. Draw yarn through rem sts and cinch closed.

Finishing

Weave in ends. Steam- or wet-block socks to finished measurements.

LINDEN PILLOW

Linden's single-pattern panel features graceful leaves alternating on each side of a straight stem. I love how each curved leaf is outlined in stitches that tilt to follow the leaves' contours.

Finished measurements
15¾" [40 cm] wide and 17¾" [45 cm] deep, with flap folded over and buttoned;
to fit an 18" [45.5 cm] square pillow form

Yarn
Lark by Quince & Co
(100% American wool; 134yd [123m]/50g)
- 4 skeins Fjord 138

Needles
- One 29" circular needle (circ) in size US 8 [5 mm]
- One spare circ in size US 8 [5 mm]
- One 24" circ in size US 7 [4.5 mm]

Or size to obtain gauge
Notions
- Waste yarn
- Stitch markers (m)
- Cable needle (cn)
- Tapestry needle
- Six 7/8" [22 mm] buttons
- One 18" [45.5 cm] square pillow form

Gauge
16 sts and 24 rnds = 4" [10 cm] in reverse stockinette stitch with larger needle, after blocking.

Special abbreviations
LC (left cross): Sl 1 st onto cable needle (cn) and hold in front, k1, then k1 from cn.
LPC (left purl cross): Sl 1 st onto cn and hold in front, p1, then k1 from cn.
RC (right cross): Sl 1 st onto cn and hold in back, k1, then k1 from cn.
RPC (right purl cross): Sl 1 st onto cn and hold in back, k1, then p1 from cn.

Tree set up panel (18 sts)
See also chart, page 106.
Rnd 1: P8, k2, p8.
Rnds 2 and 3: Rep Rnd 1.
Rnd 4: P8, k1, LC, p7.
Rnd 5: P8, k2, LC, p6.
Rnd 6: P8, k1, (LC) two times, p5.
Rnd 7: P8, k4, LC, p4.
Rnd 8: P8, k2, LPC, k1, LC, p3.
Rnd 9: P8, k2, p1, k3, LC, p2.
Rnd 10: P7, RC, k1, p1, LPC, k3, p2.
Rnd 11: P6, RC, k2, p2, k4, p2.
Rnd 12: P5, (RC) two times, k1, p2, LPC, k2, p2.

Tree panel (18 sts)
See also chart, page 106.
Rnd 1: P4, RC, k4, p3, k3, p2.
Rnd 2: P3, RC, k1, RPC, k2, p3, LPC, k1, p2.
Rnd 3: P2, RC, k3, p1, k2, p4, k2, p2.
Rnd 4: P2, k3, RPC, p1, k1, LC, p3, LPC, p2.
Rnd 5: P2, k4, p2, k2, LC, p6.
Rnd 6: P2, k2, RPC, p2, k1, (LC) two times, p5.
Rnd 7: P2, k3, p3, k4, LC, p4.
Rnd 8: P2, k1, RPC, p3, k2, LPC, k1, LC, p3.
Rnd 9: P2, k2, p4, k2, p1, k3, LC, p2.
Rnd 10: P2, RPC, p3, RC, k1, p1, LPC, k3, p2.
Rnd 11: P6, RC, k2, p2, k4, p2.
Rnd 12: P5, (RC) two times, k1, p2, LPC, k2, p2.
Rep Rnds 1-12 for tree panel.

Tree top panel (18 sts)

See also chart, page 106.
Rnd 1: P6, RC, RPC, p2, k4, p2.
Rnd 2: P5, RC, RPC, p3, LPC, k2, p2.
Rnd 3: P4, RC, k2, p5, k3, p2.
Rnd 4: P3, RC, k1, RPC, p5, LPC, k1, p2.
Rnd 5: P2, RC, k3, p7, k2, p2.
Rnd 6: P2, k3, RPC, p7, LPC, p2.
Rnd 7: P2, k4, p12.
Rnd 8: P2, k2, RPC, p12.
Rnd 9: P2, k3, p13.
Rnd 10: P2, k1, RPC, p13.
Rnd 11: P2, k2, p14.
Rnd 12: P2, RPC, p14.

Notes

1. Pillow is knitted in the round from the bottom up. Stitches for back are then bound off, and front is continued, creating a flap that is folded over and buttoned at back.
2. I prefer my pillows a little less plump, so I took some stuffing out for a flatter, softer feel.

PILLOW

With larger circular needle (circ) and using the waste yarn cast on (see page 117), CO 130 sts. Do not join.
Set up row: (RS) With working yarn, p40, place marker (pm) for panel, p8, k2, p8, pm for panel, purl to end. Pm for beg of rnd and join to work in the rnd, being careful not to twist sts.

Begin reverse stockinette and tree pattern

First rnd: Purl to marker, work Rnd 1 of tree set up panel, purl to end.
Cont in patts as est through Rnd 12 of tree set up panel.
Next rnd: Cont as est, working Rnd 1 of tree panel.
Cont in patts as est until Rnds 1-12 of tree panel have been worked a total of 3 times, then work Rnds 1-10 one more time.
Next rnd: Cont as est, working Rnd 1 of tree top panel.
Cont as est through Rnd 12 of tree top panel.
Next rnd: Purl to end, removing panel markers. Work even in rev St st until pc meas 17¾" [45 cm] from beg.
Next row: P65, bind off (see page 118) rem sts to end.
Change to smaller circ.

Begin flap

Begin working back and forth in rows.
Next row: (WS) Knit.
Cont in garter st as est until pc meas 3" [7.5 cm] from beg of flap, ending after a WS row.
Next row *buttonhole row 1:* (RS) K9, (k2tog, yo2, k7) 6 times, k2.
Next row *buttonhole row 2:* *Knit to first buttonhole, knit into yo, dropping extra wrap; rep from * for each buttonhole, knit to end.
Cont in garter st for 1" [2.5 cm] more, ending after a RS row.
Next row: (WS) Bind off knitwise.

Finishing

Weave in ends. Steam- or wet-block pillow to finished measurements.
Pick out the waste yarn cast on (see page 117) and place first 65 CO sts onto larger circ, then place rem 65 CO sts onto spare circ. With RS together, and using the three-needle bind off (see page 118), BO all sts.
Sew buttons onto back of pillow, opposite buttonholes.

Tree set up panel

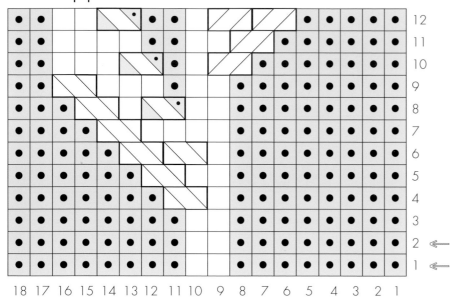

18 17 16 15 14 13 12 11 10 9 8 7 6 5 4 3 2 1

Key

	knit
•	purl
◩	LPC
◪	RPC
◿	LC
◹	RC

Tree panel

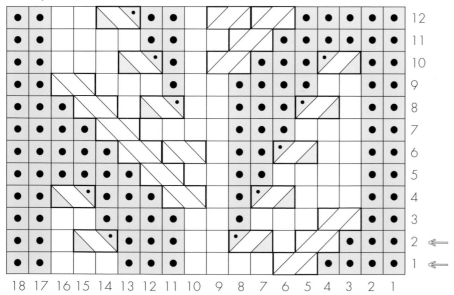

18 17 16 15 14 13 12 11 10 9 8 7 6 5 4 3 2 1

Tree top panel

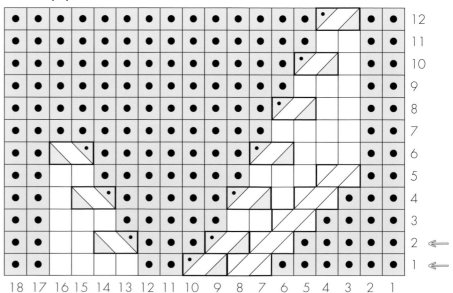

18 17 16 15 14 13 12 11 10 9 8 7 6 5 4 3 2 1

ALDER PILLOW

Knitted stitch patterns are endlessly satisfying to swatch. Their nature changes with the materials you choose: Thin yarns make delicate, etched patterns, thicker yarns make bold motifs. After knitting a pair of mitts using this simple branch pattern, I decided to use it on a larger scale on a simple pillow.

Finished measurements
17¾" [45 mm] wide and 18" [45.5 cm] deep; to fit a 20" [51 cm] square pillow form

Yarn
Puffin by Quince & Co
(100% American wool; 112yd [102m]/100g)
- 4 skeins Twig 119

Needles
- One 24" circular needle (circ) in size US 10½ [6.5 mm]
- One spare circ in size US 10½ [6.5 mm]

Or size to obtain gauge

Notions
- Stitch markers (m)
- Cable needle (cn)
- Tapestry needle
- One 20" [51 cm] square pillow form

Gauge
11¼ sts and 18 rows = 4" [10 cm] in reverse stockinette stitch, after blocking.

Special abbreviations
TRC-p (cross twisted stitch right over purl): Slip 1 st to cable needle (cn) and hold in back, k1-tbl, then p1 from cn.
TLC-p (cross twisted stitch left over purl): Slip 1 st to cn and hold in front, p1, then k1-tbl from cn.
TRC (twisted stitch right cross): Slip 1 st to cn and hold in back, k1-tbl, then k1-tbl from cn.
TLC (twisted stitch left cross): Slip 1 st to cn and hold in front, k1-tbl, then k1-tbl from cn.

Branch set up panel (15 sts)
See also chart, page 110.
Row 1: (RS) P8, TRC, p5.
Row 2: K5, (p1-tbl) two times, k8.
Row 3: P7, TRC, TLC-p, p4.
Row 4: K4, p1-tbl, k1, (p1-tbl) two times, k7.
Row 5: P6, TRC, (TLC-p) two times, p3.
Row 6: K3, (p1-tbl, k1) two times, (p1-tbl) two times, k6.

Branch panel (15 sts)
See also chart, page 110.
Row 1: (RS) P5, TRC-p, (TLC-p) three times, p2.
Row 2: K2, (p1-tbl, k1) two times, p1-tbl, k2, p1-tbl, k5.
Row 3: P5, k1-tbl, p2, (TLC-p) three times, p1.
Row 4: (K1, p1-tbl) three times, k3, p1-tbl, k5.
Row 5: P5, TLC, p2, (TLC-p) two times, p2.
Row 6: K2, p1-tbl, k1, p1-tbl, k3, (p1-tbl) two times, k5.
Row 7: P4, TRC-p, TLC, p2, TLC-p, p3.
Row 8: K3, p1-tbl, k3, (p1-tbl) two times, k1, p1-tbl, k4.
Row 9: P3, (TRC-p) two times, TLC, p6.
Row 10: K6, (p1-tbl) two times, (k1, p1-tbl) two times, k3.
Row 11: P2, (TRC-p) three times, TLC-p, p5.
Row 12: K5, p1-tbl, k2, (p1-tbl, k1) two times, p1-tbl, k2.
Row 13: P1, (TRC-p) three times, p1, TRC, p5.
Row 14: K5, (p1-tbl) two times, k2, (p1-tbl, k1) three times.

Row 15: P2, (TRC-p) two times, p1, TRC, TLC-p, p4.
Row 16: K4, p1-tbl, k1, (p1-tbl) two times, k2, p1-tbl, k1, p1-tbl, k2.
Row 17: P3, TRC-p, p1, TRC, (TLC-p) two times, p3.
Row 18: K3, (p1-tbl, k1) two times, (p1-tbl) two times, k2, p1-tbl, k3.
Rep Rows 1-18 for branch panel.

Branch top panel (15 sts)
See also chart, page 110.
Row 1: (RS) P3, (TRC-p) two times, k1-tbl, p7.
Row 2: K7, (p1-tbl, k1) two times, p1-tbl, k3.
Row 3: P2, (TRC-p) three times, p7.
Row 4: K8, (p1-tbl, k1) two times, p1-tbl, k2.
Row 5: P1, (TRC-p) three times, p8.
Row 6: K9, (p1-tbl, k1) three times.
Row 7: P2, (TRC-p) two times, p9.
Row 8: K10, p1-tbl, k1, p1-tbl, k2.
Row 9: P3, TRC-p, p10.
Row 10: K11, p1-tbl, k3.

Notes
1. Pillow is knitted flat, from the bottom up, for front, then stitches are picked up in the CO edge and worked up for back. Sides are seamed RS to WS to create an exposed edge, then pillow form is inserted and top is closed using the three-needle bind off.
2. I prefer my pillows a little less plump, so I took some stuffing out for a flatter, softer feel.

PILLOW
Front
Using the long tail cast on (see page 116), CO 50 sts. Do not join.

First row: (RS) Purl.
Next row *place markers:* K9, place marker (pm), k5, p1-tbl, k9, pm, knit to end.

Begin reverse stockinette and branch pattern
Next row: (RS) Purl to marker, work Row 1 of branch set up panel, purl to end.
Cont in patts as est through Row 6 of branch set up panel.
Next row: (RS) Cont as est, working Row 1 of branch panel.
Cont in patts as est until Rows 1-18 of branch panel have been worked a total of 2 times, then work Rows 1-8 one more time.
Next row: (RS) Cont as est, working Row 1 of branch top panel.
Cont as est through Row 10 of branch top panel.
Next row: (RS) Purl to end, removing markers.
Work even in rev St st as est until pillow meas 18" [45.5 cm] from beg, ending after a WS row.
Break yarn. Place sts onto holder or waste yarn.

Back
With WS of pillow front facing, pick up and knit 1 st in each CO st—50 sts on needle.

First row: (RS) Purl.
Next row: Knit.
Cont in rev St st until pillow meas 18" [45.5 cm] from beg (or same number of rows as for front), ending after a WS row.
Break yarn, leaving a 60" [152.5 cm] tail. Place sts onto holder or waste yarn.

Finishing
Weave in ends. Steam- or wet-block pillow to finished measurements.
Fold pillow in half along bottom edge so that WS are together. Seam the side edges of the pillow using the mattress stitch (see page 119), alternating running threads from WS of front and RS of back to create an exposed seam along edge. Insert pillow form into pillow.
Place sts for pillow back and front onto two circular needles. With WS together and yarn attached on pillow back, using the three-needle bind off (see page 118), BO all sts.

Branch set up panel

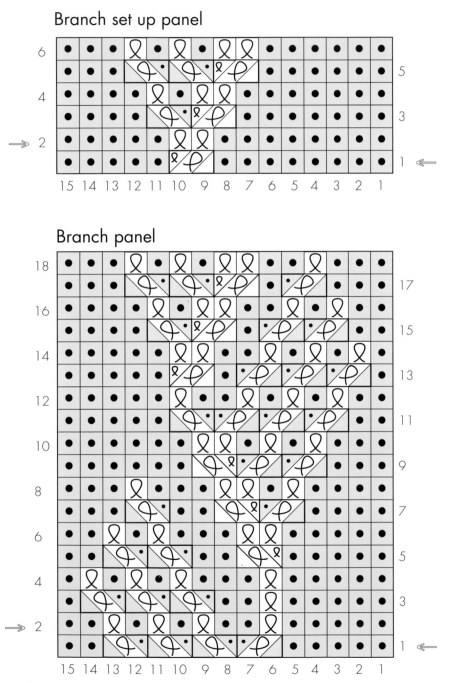

Branch panel

Key

| | purl on RS, knit on WS |

 k1-tbl on RS, p1-tbl on WS

 TRC

 TLC

 TRC-p

TLC-p

Branch top panel

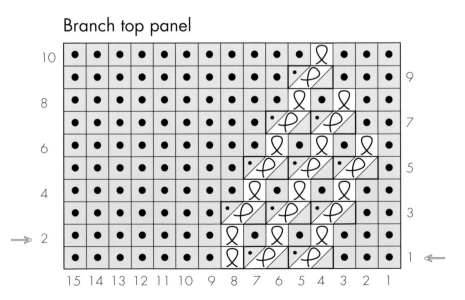

110

EDITH CARDIGAN

Edith is a long, slender cardigan with deep pockets. The sweater is really just two rectangles—one cut down the center—with sleeves. It has no buttons, and because the fronts meet at the center back neck, the borders gently hug the neck. Deep ribs at the bottom and a textured rib stitch along the center front edges keep them from rolling. The sleeves are extra long to keep the wrists warm. Roll the cuffs up when you want your hands free, roll them down to be cozy and warm.

Finished measurements

41¼ (45, 47½, 51, 53¾, 56½, 60, 62¾)" [105 (114.5, 120.5, 129.5, 136.5, 143.5, 152.5, 159.5) cm] at bust;

shown in size 45" [114.5 cm] with 12" [30.5 cm] of positive ease

Yarn

Owl by Quince & Co

(50% American wool, 50% alpaca; 120yd [110m]/50g)

- 12 (13, 14, 15, 15, 16, 17, 18) skeins Abyssinian 309

Needles

- One 32" circular needle (circ) in size US 9 [5.5 mm]
- One spare circ in size US 9 [5.5 mm]
- One set double-pointed needles in size US 9 [5.5 mm]

Or size to obtain gauge

Notions

- Stitch markers (m)
- Stitch holders or waste yarn
- Tapestry needle

Gauge

18 sts and 25 rows = 4" [10 cm] in stockinette stitch, after blocking.

Special abbreviations

sl 1 wyif: Slip 1 st purlwise with yarn in front.
sl 1 wyib: Slip 1 st purlwise with yarn in back.

Notes

Cardigan is knitted from the bottom up, in one piece, to arm opening, then fronts and back are worked separately. Shoulders are joined using the three-needle bind off. Sleeve sts are picked up around the arm opening and worked in the round to the cuff. Patch pockets are sewn on at the end.

CARDIGAN

Begin at hem

With circular needle (circ) and using the long tail cast on (see page 116), CO 182 (198, 210, 226, 238, 250, 266, 278) sts. Do not join.

Begin front and ribbed borders

First row: (RS) Sl 1 wyib, [k2, p2] 4 (4, 4, 5, 5, 5, 6, 6) times, k2, p1, place marker (pm), *k2, p2; rep from * to last 22 (22, 22, 26, 26, 26, 30, 30) sts, k2, pm, p1, [k2, p2] 4 (4, 4, 5, 5, 5, 6, 6) times, k3.

Next row: (WS) Sl 1 wyif, p1, [k2, p2] 4 (4, 4, 5, 5, 5, 6, 6) times, k2, slip marker (sl m), *p2, k2; rep from * to marker (m), sl m, [k2, p2] 5 (5, 5, 6, 6, 6, 7, 7) times to end.

Cont in patts as est until pc meas 4½" [11.5 cm] from beg, ending after a WS row.

Begin stockinette and continue front rib

Next row: (RS) Sl 1 wyib, work in textured rib as est to m, knit to next m, work textured rib to end.

Next row: Sl 1 wyif, work in patt to m, purl to next m, work in patt to end.

Cont in patts as est until pc meas 25" [63.5 cm] from beg, ending after a RS row.

Next row *inc row:* (WS) Work as est across 46 (50, 53, 57, 60, 63, 67, 70) sts for front, pm for side, k25 (29, 32, 32, 35, 38, 38, 41) sts, m1-p, pm for back ribbed panel, k20 (20, 20, 24, 24, 24, 28, 28), m1-p, k20 (20, 20, 24, 24, 24, 28, 28) sts, pm for back ribbed panel, m1-p, k25 (29, 32, 32, 35, 38, 38, 41) sts, pm for side, work as est to end (3 st inc'd)—185 (201, 213, 229, 241, 253, 269, 281) sts.

Begin back ribbed-pattern panel

Next row: (RS) Work as est to back panel m, p1, *k2, p2; rep from * to next m, work as est to end.

Next row: Work as est to back panel m, k1, *p2, k2; rep from * to next m, work as est to end. Cont as est, working in St st, with textured rib patt at center fronts and between markers at back, until pc meas 27" [68.5 cm] from beg, ending after a WS row.

Separate fronts and back

Next row: (RS) Work sts for right front to side m as est, then place these sts onto holder or waste yarn, work sts for back to next side m, then place rem sts for left front onto second holder or waste yarn—93 (101, 107, 115, 121, 127, 135, 141) sts rem on needle.

Cont working on back sts only.

Back

Next row: (WS) Using the backward loop cast on (see page 116), CO 1 st, work in patts as est to end, turn work, CO 1 st—95 (103, 109, 117, 123, 129, 137, 143) sts.

Work even in patts as est until pc meas 5¼ (5½, 5¾, 6, 6¼, 6¾, 7¼, 8)" [13.5 (14, 14.5, 15, 16, 17, 18.5, 20.5) cm], ending after a RS row. Break yarn. Place sts onto holder or waste yarn.

Left front

With RS facing, return 46 (50, 53, 57, 60, 63, 67, 70) sts for left front to circ and attach yarn.

Next row: (RS) Using the backward loop cast on, CO 1 st, work to end as est—47 (51, 54, 58, 61, 64, 68, 71) sts.

Work even in patts as est until pc meas 5¼ (5½, 5¾, 6, 6¼, 6¾, 7¼, 8)" [13.5 (14, 14.5, 15, 16, 17, 18.5, 20.5) cm], ending after a RS row. Break yarn. Place sts onto holder or waste yarn.

Right front

With WS facing, return 46 (50, 53, 57, 60, 63, 67, 70) sts for right front to circ and join yarn.

Next row: (WS) Using the knitted cast on (see page 116), CO 1 st, work to end as est—47 (51, 54, 58, 61, 64, 68, 71) sts.

Work even in patts as est until pc meas 5¼ (5½, 5¾, 6, 6¼, 6¾, 7¼, 8)" [13.5 (14, 14.5, 15, 16, 17, 18.5, 20.5) cm], ending after a RS row.

Join shoulders

Return sts for back to spare circ. With RS together, beg at right arm opening, and using the three-needle bind off (see page 118), BO all right front sts with corresponding back sts. BO (see page 118) 1 back st, return last BO st to LH needle. Return sts for left front to circ. With RS together, and using the three-needle bind off, BO left front sts with rem back sts.

Gently steam-block sweater.

Sleeves

With double-pointed needles, RS facing, and beg at underarm, pick up and knit 24 (25, 26, 27, 28, 30, 33, 36) sts to shoulder, then pick up and knit 24 (25, 26, 27, 28, 30, 33, 36) sts back to underarm (approx 3 sts for every 4 rows)—48 (50, 52, 54, 56, 60, 66, 72) sts on needle. Pm for beg of rnd.

First rnd: Knit.

Cont in St st until sleeve meas 2" [2.5 cm] from pick up.

Begin sleeve decreases

Next rnd *dec rnd*: K1, k2tog, knit to last 3 sts, ssk, k1 (2 sts dec'd)—46 (48, 50, 52, 54, 58, 64, 70) sts rem.

Rep *dec rnd* every 16 (12, 10, 12, 10, 8, 6, 6) rnds 3 (4, 4, 4, 4, 3, 8, 2) more times, then every 0 (0, 8, 0, 8, 6, 0, 4) rnds 0 (0, 1, 0, 1, 4, 0, 9) more times—40 (40, 40, 44, 44, 44, 48, 48) sts rem.

Work even in St st until sleeve meas 13½" [34 cm] from pick up.

Begin cuff

Next rnd: *K2, p2; rep from * to end.

Cont in rib as est until sleeve meas 18" [46 cm] from pick up.

Next rnd: Loosely bind off in patt.

Rep for other sleeve.

Pockets (make 2)

With circ and using the long tail cast on, CO 38 sts. Do not join.

First row: (RS) Knit.

Work in St st until pocket meas 6" [15 cm], ending after a WS row.

Begin rib

Next row: (RS) *K2, p2; rep from *, end k2.

Next row: *P2, k2; rep from *, end p2.

Work in rib as est for 1" [2.5 cm], ending after a WS row.

Next row: (RS) Loosely bind off in patt.

Finishing

Weave in ends. Steam- or wet-block cardigan and pockets to finished measurements.
Place pockets so that the CO edge lines up with the top of the bottom ribbing, and the side edge is 1¾ (2¾, 3¼, 3¼, 4, 4¾, 4¾, 5¼)" [4.5 (7, 8.5, 8.5, 10, 12, 12, 13.5) cm] from the edge of the textured rib. (Pocket is centered between front and back at side.) Sew pockets in place using the mattress stitch (see page 119).

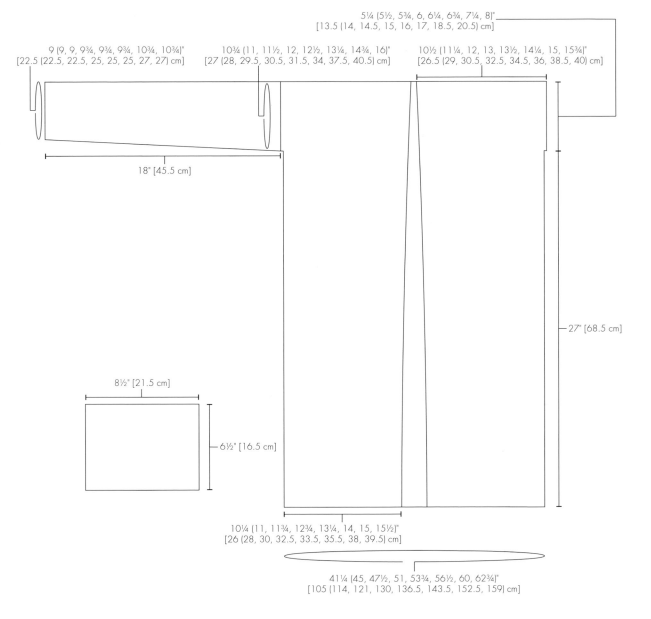

5¼ (5½, 5¾, 6, 6¼, 6¾, 7¼, 8)"
[13.5 (14, 14.5, 15, 16, 17, 18.5, 20.5) cm]

9 (9, 9, 9¾, 9¾, 9¾, 10¾, 10¾)"
[22.5 (22.5, 22.5, 25, 25, 25, 27, 27) cm]

10¾ (11, 11½, 12, 12½, 13¼, 14¾, 16)"
[27 (28, 29.5, 30.5, 31.5, 34, 37.5, 40.5) cm]

10½ (11¼, 12, 13, 13½, 14¼, 15, 15¾)"
[26.5 (29, 30.5, 32.5, 34.5, 36, 38.5, 40) cm]

18" [45.5 cm]

27" [68.5 cm]

8½" [21.5 cm]

6½" [16.5 cm]

10¼ (11, 11¾, 12¾, 13¼, 14, 15, 15½)"
[26 (28, 30, 32.5, 33.5, 35.5, 38, 39.5) cm]

41¼ (45, 47½, 51, 53¾, 56½, 60, 62¾)"
[105 (114, 121, 130, 136.5, 143.5, 152.5, 159) cm]

Stockinette stitch (St st)

Flat
Knit on the RS, purl on the WS.
In the round
Knit every round.

Reverse stockinette stitch (rev St st)

Flat
Purl on the RS, knit on the WS.
In the round
Purl every round.

Garter stitch

Flat
Knit every row.
In the round
Rnd 1: Purl.
Rnd 2: Knit.

CASTING ON

Backward loop cast on

*Wrap yarn around left thumb from front to back and secure in palm with other fingers. Insert RH needle upward through strand on thumb. Slip loop from thumb onto needle, gently pulling yarn to tighten. Rep from * for desired number of sts.

Cable cast on

*Insert RH needle between the first and second sts on the LH needle as if to knit and draw a loop through, then slip the new st from the RH to LH needle, casting on 1 st. Rep from * for desired number of sts.

German twisted (also known as Old Norwegian) cast on

This cast on begins the same as for the long tail version. Measure your long tail and make a slip knot.

Create your thumb loop in the same way, but instead of inserting the needle upward into the loop, work as follows:

Step 1: Bring needle under both strands formed by the thumb loop, then draw the needle down into the loop, grabbing the back strand. The result is a loop on the needle, with the strand leading from the needle to thumb resting behind the strand leading to the long tail. Secure this position by grabbing the needle with your left hand while it is still in the loop on your thumb.

Step 2: With your right hand, wrap the working yarn counter-clockwise around the needle and sandwich it between the thumb and the needle in your left hand.

Step 3: Grasp the needle with your right hand. Bend your thumb slightly downward, allowing the loop to become uncrossed, then draw the needle tip down into the loop, and remove your thumb. Pull gently on the tail to firm up your stitch.

Rep Steps 1-3 for desired number of stitches.

Knitted cast on

*Insert RH needle into the first st on the LH needle as if to knit and draw a loop through, but instead of dropping the old st off the LH needle, slip the new st from the RH to LH needle, casting on 1 st. Rep from * for desired number of sts.

Long tail cast on

Set Up: To work this cast on you will need a long tail of yarn. The general rule of thumb for determining how long to make the tail is to allow for approx ½ an inch of yarn per stitch to be cast on. A quick way to do this is to wrap the yarn around the needle 10 times (to approximate 10 stitches worth) take that length of yarn and multiply according to number of stitches you need to cast on (remembering that each length is worth 10 stitches). Once you have your tail make a slipknot and place onto the needle. Position the strands so the tail is on the left and working yarn is on the right. Hold the needle and the working yarn in your right hand, the tail in your left.

Step 1: Grab the tail with your left hand a few inches away from the needle, holding it in a loose fist with your palm facing downward. Your thumb should be over the yarn. Loop the tail around your thumb by rotating your thumb around the yarn from behind, then toward you (go first over, then under, then position your thumb upright, palm facing). The result is a loop on your thumb with strand attached to the needle crossing over the strand leading to the long tail.

Step 2: Insert the tip of the needle upward into the loop. Secure this position by grabbing the needle with your left hand while it is still in the loop on your thumb.

Step 3: With your right hand, bring the working yarn behind the needle and wrap it counter-clockwise around the needle, then sandwich it between the thumb and the needle in your left hand.

Step 4: Grasp the needle with your right hand. Lift the loop of yarn that's been sitting on your left thumb, bringing it back and over the tip of the needle. Pull gently on the tail to firm up your stitch.

Rep Steps 1-4 for desired number of stitches, counting the slip knot as one stitch.

Waste yarn cast on
Using smooth waste yarn of the same weight or slightly smaller than the working yarn, cast on using the long tail cast on.

Picking out a waste yarn cast on
Beginning at the end of the cast on row, pick up each st of the first row in the working yarn by inserting the needle from front to back, lifting the right leg of the st up and onto the needle. Once all stitches are on the needle carefully unpick or cut the waste yarn, and gently pull it out, leaving the first row of the working yarn on the needle.

SHORT ROWS
German short row
Make double stitch
(RS and WS) Beginning with yarn to the front of RH needle, slip first st on LH needle purlwise. Bring yarn up and over RH needle, tightening this st and causing the st from the row below to rise up on needle, appearing as if it were 2 sts (referred to as a double stitch). Cont as instructed for your pattern, maintaining this double stitch.

Working into a double stitch (k1 double st/p1 double st)
Insert needle through both parts of the double st and knit or purl them together as one st.

Japanese (also known as Sunday) short row
Place a locking stitch marker
(RS and WS) Work as instructed in your pattern. After turning your work, place a locking stitch marker around the working yarn (or drape a strand of waste yarn over it), then continue to work as instructed, letting the marker act as a placeholder.

Picking up the loop
(RS) Work to the turning point (you'll see a gap), then gently pull on the marker or waste yarn, bringing up a loop. Place this loop onto the LH needle, remove the marker, then knit the loop together with the next st.
(WS) Work to the turning point (you'll see a gap), slip the next st purlwise to the RH needle (the stitch just after the gap), then gently pull on the locking stitch marker or waste yarn, bringing up a loop. Place this loop onto the LH needle, remove the marker, then return the slipped stitch to the LH needle and purl it together with the loop.

Note: Instructions unique to each pattern explain how to work the final set of short rows when working in the round.

Wrap and turn (w&t)
On the knit side
Slip next st to the RH needle and bring yarn between needles to the front of work. Return slipped st to the LH needle. Turn work and bring yarn between needles to front, ready to work next WS row.
On the purl side
Slip next st to the RH needle and bring yarn between needles to the back of the work. Return slipped st to the LH needle. Turn work and bring yarn between needles to back, ready to work next RS row.

Picking up wraps
In stockinette stitch
(RS) Insert the right needle tip into the wrap from below, front to back, then into the stitch that it wraps, and knit the two together, making sure that the wrap falls to the wrong side of the work.
(WS) Insert the right needle tip into the wrap from below, back to front, lifting it over the stitch that it wraps, and purl the two together, making sure that the wrap falls to the wrong side of work.

In reverse stockinette stitch
(RS) Slip wrapped st to RH needle. Insert LH needle tip from below, into wrap, then into the wrapped st, and purl the two together.
(WS) Insert the right needle tip into the wrap from below, front to back, then into the stitch that it wraps, and knit the two together.

KNITTING SMALL CIRCUMFERENCES

Using double-pointed needles (dpns)

Cast the number of sts required for your project onto one dpn. Rearrange the sts evenly (or as indicated in your pattern) onto each dpn. Join to work in the rnd, being careful not to twist sts. Using the empty dpn as the RH needle, work the sts on the first needle as indicated for your project. When all of the sts on that needle have been worked, use the needle you've just emptied to work the sts on the next needle. Continue in this manner, working the sts on one needle, then using the newly emptied needle to work the sts on the next.

Using two circular needles (circs)

Cast the number of sts required for your project onto one circ. Rearrange the sts onto two circs as indicated in your pattern. Only one circ is used at a time, so once you've rearranged your sts over two needles, let the sts not currently being worked rest on the cable of the circ not in use. Join to work in the round, being careful not to twist sts. *With the first set of sts pushed to LH needle tip of the circ they are sitting on, use the other tip of that same circ as the RH needle, and work the sts on the first needle as indicated for your project. When all of the sts on that needle have been worked, turn your knitting around and rep from * for second circ, until you reach the end of the round. Continue in this manner to work in the round on two circular needles.

BINDING OFF

Basic bind off

Work 2 sts in pattern as established, then *pass the first st worked over the next st to bind off 1 st. Work 1 more st from the LH needle; rep from * for desired number of sts.

If binding off to the end of a row, rep from * until 1 st remains on the LH needle. Break yarn and draw through remaining st, leaving a 6-8" [15-20.5 cm] tail for weaving in ends.

Three-needle bind off

Hold the needles parallel with points aligned. With a third needle, knit the first st of front and back needles together, *knit next st from each needle together (2 sts on RH needle), lift the first st over the second st and off the RH needle to bind off 1 st; rep from * until all sts are bound off. Break yarn and draw through remaining st, leaving a 6-8" [15-20.5 cm] tail for weaving in.

GRAFTING

Grafting live purl stitches to rows

Leave live sts on thin, smooth waste yarn. Locate the center of the rows to be grafted (at the shoulder seam, if working a sweater).

Locate the center of the live sts (equal number of sts each for left and right halves). Thread tapestry needle with yarn at least double the length of your grafting job.

First half

Leave half the length of yarn as a tail at the center of the work to graft the right half.

Lay pieces on a flat surface, the piece with live sts closer to you, and the side edge of the second piece farther away, with live stitches facing the rows of the side edge.

Step 1: Draw yarn as if to knit through the first st to the left of center.

Step 2: Draw yarn through the first running thread to the left of center.

Step 3: Draw yarn as if to purl through the same live st.

Work Steps 1-3 one at a time, taking care not to draw the yarn too tightly.

Continue in this manner, working to the left, away from the center, and skipping running threads as instructed in your pattern until all live sts have been grafted to rows. Leave yarn here to work the next step of finishing for your pattern.

Second half

Turn work around so the side edge is closer to you. Live sts are now upside down. Use the long tail at center.

Step 1: Draw yarn from the top down (purlwise, from this perspective) through the first st to the left of center.

Step 2: Draw yarn through the first running thread to the left of center.

Step 3: Draw yarn up (knitwise, from this perspective) through the same live st.

Work Steps 1-3 one at a time, taking care not to draw the yarn too tightly.

Continue in this manner, working to the left, away from the center, and skipping running threads as instructed in your pattern until all live sts have been grafted to rows. Leave yarn here to work the next step of finishing for your pattern.

SEAMING

Mattress stitch

Place edges to be seamed side by side, with RS or WS facing up, as indicated for your pattern. Thread tapestry needle with yarn at least double the length of your seaming job.

Set up: Beginning with piece on the right, insert needle up from under the piece, between the lower edge and the first running thread, one st away from the side edge. Rep for piece on the left, draw yarn up, cinching the two pieces together, and leaving a tail to weave in later.

For side edges

Step 1: Locate the point where the yarn is coming up from below on the right piece. Starting here, insert needle under next running thread and draw yarn through and gently cinch to join to left piece.

Step 2: Locate the point where the yarn is coming up from below on the left piece. Starting here, insert needle under next running thread and draw yarn through, gently cinching to join to right piece.

Rep Steps 1 and 2 until pieces are joined. Note that yarn will always begin and end on the top side of fabric. If you are seaming pieces that do not have the same number of rows, occasionally work two running threads at a time for the longer piece, then resume working one-to-one. Continue checking and working two-to-one periodically if one piece continues to be longer.

For CO or BO edges

Step 1: Locate the point where the yarn is coming up from below on the right piece. Starting here, insert needle under next whole st (this will be two legs, forming a "v" shape either facing toward or away from the edge), draw yarn through and gently cinch to join to left piece.

Step 2: Locate the point where the yarn is coming up from below on the left piece. Starting here, insert needle under next whole st, and draw yarn through, gently cinching to join to right piece.

Rep Steps 1 and 2 until pieces are joined. Note that yarn will always begin and end on the top side of fabric.

Mattress stitch for a side edge to a BO edge

Place edges to be seamed side by side, with RS facing up. Thread tapestry needle with yarn at least double the length of your seaming job.

Set up: Beginning with the BO edge, insert needle up from the WS into the center of the first BO st. On the side edge, insert needle from the WS up, between the lower edge and the first running thread, one st away from the side edge. Draw yarn up, cinching the two pcs together, and leaving a tail to weave in later.

Step 1: Locate the point where the yarn is coming up from below on the BO edge. Starting here, insert needle under next whole st (this will be two legs, forming a "v" shape either facing toward or away from the edge), draw yarn through and gently cinch to join to side edge.

Step 2: Locate the point where the yarn is coming up from below on the side edge. With pieces laying flat, seaming edges together, assess how many running threads you will need to pass under to "catch up" to where you've left off on the BO edge (usually 1 or 2 running threads). Starting at the point where the yarn is coming up from the last action on this side, insert needle under the appropriate number of running threads and draw yarn through, gently cinching to join to BO edge.

Rep Steps 1 and 2, assessing each time how many running threads to work to keep the edges lining up nicely, until pieces are joined. Note that yarn will always begin and end on the top side of fabric.

SPECIAL ABBREVIATIONS

k2tog: Knit 2 sts together (1 st decreased).

k3tog: Knit 3 sts together (2 sts decreased).

m1 (make 1): Insert LH needle from front to back under horizontal strand between st just worked and next st, knit lifted strand through the back loop (1 st increased).

m1-p (make 1 purlwise): Insert LH needle from front to back under horizontal strand between st just worked and next st, purl lifted strand through the back loop (1 st increased).

p2tog: Purl 2 sts together (1 st decreased).

s2kp (central double decrease): Slip 2 sts tog knitwise to the RH needle, k1, pass 2 slipped sts over knit st (2 sts decreased).

sk2p: Slip 1 st knitwise to RH needle, k2tog, pass slipped st over st created by k2tog (2 sts decreased).

ssk (slip, slip, knit): Slip 2 sts one at a time knitwise to the RH needle; return sts to LH needle in turned position and knit them together through the back loops (1 st decreased).

ssp (slip, slip, purl): Slip 2 sts one at a time knitwise to the RH needle; return sts to LH needle in turned position and purl them together through the back loops (1 st decreased).

yo (yarn over): Bring yarn between needles to the front, then over RH needle ready to knit the next st (1 st increased).

yo2: Yarn over needle twice. On the next row, knit into the first yo, dropping the second from the needle (1 st increased).

yo-inc (yarn over increase): Bring yarn over needle, making a new st. On the next row/rnd, knit or purl the yo through the back loop.

STANDARD ABBREVIATIONS

approx	approximately	patt(s)	pattern(s)
beg	begin(ning); begin; begins	pc(s)	piece(s)
BO	bind off	plm	place locking marker
BOR	beginning of round	pm	place marker
CO	cast on	rem	remain(ing)
CC	contrasting color	rep	repeat; repeating
circ	circular needle	rev St st	reverse stockinette stitch
cm	centimeter(s)	RH	right hand
cn	cable needle	rib	ribbing
cont	continue(s); continuing	rnd(s)	round(s)
dec('d)	decrease(d)	RS	right side
dpn(s)	double-pointed needle(s)	sl	slip
est	establish(ed)	sl m	slip marker
g	gram(s)	st(s)	stitch(es)
inc('d)	increase(d)	St st	stockinette stitch
k	knit	tbl	through the back loop
LH	left hand	tog	together
MC	main color	wyib	with yarn in back
meas	measures	wyif	with yarn in front
mm	millimeter(s)	WS	wrong side
m(s)	marker(s)	yd	yard(s)
p	purl		

LINKS

CASTING ON

Backward loop cast on
www.knitty.com/ISSUEfall05/FEATfall05TT.html
Cable, knitted, and long tail cast ons
www.knitty.com/ISSUEsummer05/FEATsum05TT.html
German twisted cast on
www.theshetlandtrader.com/blog/index.php/tutorials/

SHORT ROWS

German short row
www.youtube.com/watch?v=JpeRoXHPVEI
Japanese short row
www.youtube.comwatch?v=qR6IgBRcV5Y
Wrap and turn
www.knitty.com/ISSUEsummer03/FEATbonnetric.html

KNITTING SMALL CIRCUMFERENCES

Using two circular needles
www.dummies.com/how-to/content/knitting-in-the-round-with-two-circular-needles.html

BINDING OFF

Basic bind off
www.knitty.com/ISSUEsummer06/FEATsum06TT.html
Three-needle bind off
www.knitty.com/ISSUEfall06/FEATfall06TT.html

FINISHING

Mattress stitch for side edges
www.knitty.com/ISSUEspring04/mattress.html
Mattress stitch for CO or BO edges
newstitchaday.com/how-to-knit-seaming-two-bind-off-edges-together/

For other helpful tips on finishing, visit our website at quinceandco.com.

HISTORY & BIO

Quince & Co is a handknitting yarn and knitwear design company launched in 2010 by Pam Allen in partnership with a historic spinning mill in Maine. Our goal is to work as much as possible with American fibers and mills and, when we can't have a yarn made to our specifications in the US, we look for suppliers overseas who make yarn in as earth- and labor-friendly a way as possible.

Quince began with a core line of five wool yarns—Finch, Chickadee, Lark, Osprey, and Puffin—each with its own personality, each in 37 colors, and all spun in the US from American wool. Today Quince & Co's core line comes in 53 colors and we've added Tern, a silk/wool blend, Owl, an alpaca/wool blend, and Piper, a super fine mohair/ merino blend sourced specifically from Texas. In addition, Quince makes two organic linen yarns, Sparrow and Kestrel, with a mill in Italy. Find out more at www.quinceandco.com.

Pam Allen has worked in the knitting industry for many years as an independent hand-knitwear designer, editor-in-chief of Interweave Knits magazine, and creative director at Classic Elite Yarns. She is the author of Knitting for Dummies (John Wiley & Sons, 2002) and Scarf Style (Interweave Press, 2004).

ACKNOWLEDGEMENTS

Many thanks to the talented and hard-working crew at Quince & Co for their help in creating this book: Jerusha Robinson, Dawn Catanzaro, and Adi Kehoe for pattern writing, knitting, tech editing, proofing, shipping, and generally keeping the project moving forward; Kristen TenDyke for tech editing; Karen Martinez for her good eye and expertise in finessing the graphics; and Ryan FitzGerald for his invaluable help at the shoot.

Thanks, too, to Mary Henley, Anne Anderson, and Heather Kiernan for sample knitting; and to Kathleen Milliken and Nick Mazuroski for modeling (and moving furniture).

We're also grateful to Bliss (blissboutiques.com) in Portland, Maine, for lending us clothes for styling, and to Franklin Printing in Farmington, Maine, powered by wind and using paper made in America whenever possible.